ESSENCE

BLACK MEN
IN THEIR
OWN WORDS

Also edited by Patricia Mignon Hinds
21st Century Sister: The Essence Five Keys to Success
Total Makeover: Body, Beauty, Spirit
ESSENCE: 25 Years of Celebrating Black Women

Selected children's books by Patricia Mignon Hinds
My Best Friend
What I Want to Be
A Day in the Life of Morgan Freeman

Books by Susan L. Taylor
In the Spirit
Lessons in Living
Confirmations (coauthor)

ESSENCE

BLACK MEN
IN THEIR
OWN WORDS

EDITED BY PATRICIA MIGNON HINDS WITH SUSAN L. TAYLOR
FOREWORD BY ED LEWIS • INTRODUCTION BY CLARENCE O. SMITH

CROWN PUBLISHERS / NEW YORK

Published by Crown Publishers, New York, New York.
Member of the Crown Publishing Group, a division of Random House, Inc.
www.randomhouse.com

CROWN is a trademark and the Crown colophon is a registered trademark of Random House, Inc.

Printed in China

Design by Elizabeth Van Itallie

Library of Congress Cataloging-in-Publication Data
Black men in their own words / edited by Patricia Mignon Hinds with Susan L. Taylor—1st ed.
    Includes index.
    1. African-American men—Biography.
    2. African-American men—Pictorial works.
    3. African-American men—Social conditions
    I. Hinds, P. Mignon. II. Taylor, Susan L.
    E185.86.B5263   2002
    920.71'089'96073—dc21   2001032505

ISBN 0-609-60366-3

10 9 8 7 6 5 4 3 2 1

First Edition

ACKNOWLEDGMENTS

So often, we don't have a platform to honor our men and to give them praise for achievements that are sometimes taken for granted in our society. Through this book I acknowledge all men who do extraordinary things to enrich our lives. But I must pay tribute to all the beautiful and supportive men— our brothers, family members, and friends—who are not in this book, but are in many ways of the same spirit and mind of those whose testaments are shared.

A profound thank-you to the wonderful men featured in this book for opening their hearts and for sharing their very personal stories and time. Special thanks to their assistants, publicists, families, and others who helped us through the process.

This remarkable book would not have been possible without the hard work and dedicated efforts of the Essence Books team: Elizabeth Entien, Teresa Fulwood, and Tiffany Hill.

Special thanks to writers Amiri Baraka and William Jelani Cobb. And I am grateful to those who played a part on our editorial support team: Mateifa Angaza, June Bryant, Janice Bryant, Angela Dodson, Robert Fleming, Sherri Holder, Edwin Smith, and Charlotte Wiggers. And thanks to the photographers whose images appear.

The precious *Essence* family are greatly appreciated for lending their ears, ideas, and insight in making this book a

reality: Jan deChabert, Monique Greenwood, LaVon Leak-Wilks, Claire McIntosh, and Robin Stone. Also thanks to Diane Weathers, Marsha Augustin, Paulette Brown, Elayne Fluker, Sharon Haynes, Katherine Leary, and Debra Parker for their support. And to Ron Bright, Gregory Boyea, Andrew Chambers, Edgerton Maloney, Larry Ramo, and Shon Weathers.

I also thank David Mills, Ellis Cose, and Greg Tate. And thanks to Damaa Bell, Jeannine Chucan, Monique DeJongh, Donna Mason, Ishan Muhammad, Knox Robinson, Michelle Strait, Sherrieann Thomas, and Tracy Ingram for providing assistance in our early stages. And to Sandra DaCosta and Steve Manning.

Many blessings to Marlene Connor and Ayesha Pande. And to Darryl Wilson, Gail Wilson, and the Wheelers.

At Crown, special appreciation to Steve Ross, Kristin Kiser, Lauren Dong, Claudia Gabel, and Rhoda Dunn, and to designer Elizabeth Van Itallie.

As always, an abundance of gratitude to Ed Lewis, Susan L. Taylor, Clarence O. Smith, and Michelle Ebanks, and to Harry Dedyo, Bill Knight, Jim Forsythe, Elaine P. Williams, and Barbara Britton.

—PATRICIA MIGNON HINDS

CONTENTS

FOREWORD
BY ED LEWIS

There is a portrait of Jackie Robinson in my office; it hangs just to the right of my desk where I can easily glance at it. That man had a profound impact on me when he entered professional baseball. I absolutely wanted to be like Jackie Robinson. This was a man who cared about his family. He was a four-letter athlete at UCLA. He earned solid B grades, ran track, played football, baseball, and basketball. I often look at that portrait and think about what Jackie Robinson was able to accomplish under incredible pressure.

He withstood all the attempts at intimidation and humiliation and still did his very best. And because he did, many of us have benefited—not only from his courage, but also from his willingness to take a stand, to be accountable, and to be an example. There are other heroes: Muhammad Ali, who walked away from boxing at the height of his physical skills rather than compromise his beliefs; Malcolm X, who taught us that there was nothing wrong with us as Black men. He told us to be proud, to take care of our communities, and not ever to let anyone defile us. Paul Robeson. Marcus Garvey. These men—and the weight of the examples they set—are the reason for *Black Men: In Their Own Words.*

This book is an opportunity for us as Black men to express ourselves about our experiences and what we care very deeply about. Family, friendship, manhood, racism, what it is to be a Black man in our society—our words, our experiences, and our collective wisdom have never been more important.

Our world has changed dramatically since we witnessed tragic deaths and massive destruction from terrorist attacks on the World Trade Center and the Pentagon. The sad truth, however, is that terrorism is nothing new to African Americans; we have known its horrible impact since those first ancestors arrived in Jamestown, Virginia, in 1619. We have lived through the terrors of lynching, mob violence, and rape—and, in the face of these trials, found ways to be hopeful and endure. Perhaps all Americans might reflect on the example of resilience, grace, and courage our Black ancestors displayed when they confronted another variety of terrorism.

We have had to overcome many obstacles—racial profiling, drugs, economic apartheid, Black-on-Black crime, and the vast numbers of Black men incarcerated. This collection is a statement about how we stick together, try to survive, take care of our families, and do the right thing. *Black Men: In Their Own Words* represents wisdom and lessons gleaned from the lives of our brothers.

My own life lessons were taught to me by family. Although I was raised in the Bronx, I spent my summers with my grandparents in Prince Edward County, Virginia. My grandparents believed that hard work killed nobody. They imparted to me the value of teamwork, of taking care of myself and my family, and the importance of education. My mother provided me with discipline, love, and oversight. She instilled caring and understanding—and toughness, too. The seeds of my wanting to work in business came from my family as well. My uncle, Tracy Spencer, had his own

business. He talked to me about having control over one's life and destiny, and told me that the only way you can have that is to have something of your own. He, too, was an example. The most significant value I learned is the importance of being responsible and accountable—not only to yourself, but also to your loved ones, and particularly to your children. Being a man is about taking care of our families and ourselves.

This book was conceived in the spirit of bearing witness. In sharing their stories, the contributors to this collection are being responsible and accountable to their communities. Their experiences, anecdotes, and memories highlight our triumphs, both great and small, and remind us that we are all here for a purpose. *Black Men: In Their Own Words* is offered as a testament to willingness to be an example, to take a stand, and to strive to be the best that we can be. Just like Jackie showed me. ■

Ed Lewis is chairman and CEO of Essence Communications.

INTRODUCTION

BY CLARENCE O. SMITH

Courage, talent, tenacity, strength, character. Years of studying our history—and my own life history—have left these virtues at the forefront of my mind, along with names like Baldwin, Ellington, and Du Bois. My words are distinctly linked to my ideas about what it means to be a Black man in America and the daily experiences that require each of us to summon up our deepest personal reserves. In too many instances, the words associated with Black men are part of a paint-by-numbers portrait of despair in our communities. Filtered through a hazy lens of public perception, other less accurate words are conjured up in relation to Black men. We know the stereotypes. The most pressing issue, however, is the words we associate with ourselves.

As the cofounder of a publishing company, I believe in the power of words. I know their potential to shape, inform, educate, and heal, as well as to destroy. As a Black man, I understand the importance of speaking our own words, unfiltered and unfettered; I recognize how essential it is to have a forum where we can freely express the thoughts and ideas we associate with ourselves.

Growing up, my dad taught me about strength and tenacity. He was not by today's standards an overwhelming success. He was a man who, like most African-American men in this country, came from extremely humble beginnings. He was highly intelligent, a keen observer of the politics,

economics, and social characteristics of America, and he had a strong sense of history. He had great pride, even as he often tasted the bitterness of rejection and racism from the larger society. He struggled hard to become an entrepreneur, though he had very few resources to draw upon. Yet he never quit.

He succumbed to a stroke at age forty-nine, joining the

ranks of so many Black men who died too soon trying to maintain their manhood while being a Black man. Even today, on the cusp of a new century, we die disproportionately from heart attack, stroke, liver failure, and drug and alcohol consumption—afflictions directly related to the stress of being Black in America.

My father's story was not atypical for many Black men of that day, but in his own way he bequeathed to his children a legacy of tenacity and pursuit of excellence. He taught us that in America, in order for Black people to achieve parity with the larger society, they would ultimately have to become producers and owners of, as opposed to merely consumers of, goods. He wanted us all to understand the importance of ownership. That lesson shaped me as I worked my way through my own life's decisions—and I don't think I ever strayed far from that vision. But somewhere along the path of struggle, the standard of excellence that I accepted as a virtue to aspire to has come to be seen as a "White thing." Our young people must not be further burdened with the additional pressures of associating academic skill with Whiteness. That is the most destructive notion of all.

Our ranks are deep with men of character and talent, individuals whose intellect, diligence, and integrity enabled them to negotiate society's minefields. Men who believed that despite the external conditions, much of what happens is still determined by how one responds individually to adversity. I think of men as diverse as Colin Powell, Arthur Ashe, Nelson Mandela, and Thurgood Marshall and recognize that they have come to the fore through resilience, talent, and depth of character. Each of them had to develop a finely honed intellect and understanding of the chess game of life in order to checkmate challenges as they came along. Anticipatory perception, analytical skill, and decisiveness are all traits common in those who have been able to achieve success.

Courage is a Martin Luther King's or a Malcolm X's taking action while knowing that they had no military power, no economic or political power, no power other than their own vision and moral force. Yet they persevered, using that moral force to transform others, bringing those less certain and less committed into the fold to move us ever forward. We've always produced men like that—from Frederick Douglass to Randall Robinson—who unflinchingly spoke truth to power and ultimately changed the world. Ours is a legacy of optimism—and the courage it took to be optimistic amid bleak conditions. That courageous optimism is a most powerful resource available to our young people.

Our choices of words may vary, but each of us has a responsibility to make our lives guideposts for our young people. The reservoir of contributions that Black men have made to this world has given me great spiritual nourishment. The words and deeds of our brothers must be understood and valued. Courage, tenacity, strength, character, and talent are my own individual frames of reference. Taken collectively, they ensure that one other word is associated with African-Americans: excellence. ■

Clarence O. Smith is president of Essence Communications.

MANHOOD

I can be the beautiful Black man
because I am
the beautiful Black man, and you, girl, child nightlove,
you are beautiful
too.
We are something, the two of us
the people love us for being
though they may call us out our
name, they love our strength
in the midst of, quiet, at the peak of,
violence, for the sake of, at the lust of
pure life, we worship the sun,

We are strange in a way because we know
who we are. Black beings passing through
a tortured passage of flesh.

—Amiri Baraka

Branford Marsalis

A member of the musical Marsalis dynasty, with roots in Louisiana jazz, saxophonist Branford Marsalis has now made his mark as a distinguished musician of contemporary jazz. In the 1980s, after stints in Art Blakey's Jazz Messengers, Clark Terry's orchestra, and his brother Wynton's quintet, he played with popular rock artist Sting before forming his own quartet. In the 1990s, he had a six-year stint heading the *Tonight Show* band. His recordings include *Requiem, Creation,* and *Contemporary Jazz.*

DESPITE ALL THAT is said and written, it is very difficult to be a man. What it means to be a man can vary depending upon who you talk to, but society has had its own ideal for centuries. Traditionally, the man has been the protector, the provider, the one responsible for the physical and financial well-being of the family. Like millions of others, I did my best to live up to that ideal for a number of years.

My first inkling that all was not well in the land of manhood was in 1989. I was in a movie theater watching *Field of Dreams.* Being a baseball fanatic, I went to the movie for the theme alone, but I was bowled over by the parallel between the timeless aesthetic of the noble sport and human spirituality, and how it all relates in the end to fathers and sons playing catch.

I derived pleasure from all that intellectualization, which appeals to only a few people, but when the movie ended, I was not prepared for what I saw. The lights came up, and I was surrounded by men in their thirties crying their eyes out. This sight made me more determined to be the ideal father, to avoid an absentee reckoning with my own son. While I saw it as a sign, it was actually a foreshadowing.

It has been said that you never know what you have in a partner until there is a crisis. I found myself mired in a divorce, struggling to process the pain associated with that failure while raising a child. At this critical time I was offered a unique career opportunity for nightly exposure, but one that required me to relocate and leave my son behind. So I did what people do: I rationalized. *This is a good career move and would be fun,* I told myself. *I'll see my son almost every weekend. It may be difficult at first, but he'll be all right. It's really for the best.* I conned the hell out of myself, and I ran.

And run I did. Every time I heard the little voice in my head, I chased it out with my skewed logic. When the weekend flights to see my son became too much to bear, the little voice would try to speak. *This is a good career move,* I would say as I chased the voice out. As my personality became more irascible, my flawed reasoning became more desperate. My son's personality became a reflection of my own, and his behavior at school became less than desirable. Nonetheless, I stayed the course, making life difficult for everyone around me.

My brother Delfeayo once told me, "Denial is easier than confrontation, especially when that which you have to confront is yourself." On the verge of insanity and not knowing what else to do, I returned to New York. On my first day back I arrived at a crossroads. Sitting on the floor of my house, I found myself too tired to fight the voice that had been in my head for more than two years. It uttered a single word: *Coward.*

There are few things in life that can justify leaving your child and moving thousands of miles away. It is not the manly thing to do. In that defining moment I realized I was not the man I wanted to be, but with that realization, I put myself on the path to becoming one.

I now work to live. I spend as much time with my family as I can, for neither they nor I will be here forever. I listen as well as talk. I lead by example, and I no longer define myself by my work or my wealth. I am far from being the man I want to be, but I know that I am a lot closer to it than I was. ■

Bill Duke

THE ISSUES OF manhood and the madness of macho are essential questions that trap all young men. Whether it's through being gangsters or making gangsta rap or believing macho men don't cry, by acting out these rituals, we attempt to define our manhood. We try to prove how much manhood we have by wearing the toughest clothes and sunglasses, driving the finest cars, beating women, having the girlfriend with the biggest breasts, and bragging about the size of our penis, how many people we've killed, how many bitches we've slapped, and all of that nonsense. It's absurd, because your manhood is not what you do, it's who you are. If you have fifty cars, fifty women, fifty suits, and plenty of gold chains, and you've shot fifteen people, it does not mean that you're a man. Your manhood is who you are beneath all that. It is the foundation of your humanity. That's what we have to start exploring in order to fill the void of individual despair.

My uncles and my father felt that I had to prove my manhood so I could survive in the real world. Because I was big when I was young, they forced me into strict gender roles: playing football and baseball, being tough—these were

Bill Duke, the critically acclaimed actor, writer, director, and producer in television, theater, and film, has garnered an impressive list of credits. He has directed and acted in several popular television series, such as *Miami Vice* and *New York Undercover,* for which he directed the pilot. His feature-film directorial credits include *Rage in Harlem, Sister Act 2: Back in the Habit,* and *Hoodlum.* His film acting credits include *Foolish* and *Always Outnumbered, Always Outgunned.* Duke established RAWWW, the new media division of his YAGYA Productions. He has written two books and has served as chair of the Department of Radio, Television, and Film at Howard University.

rituals of so-called manhood, and I hated all of them. I was not a physical person. I preferred reading and thinking.

I used to have to go fishing, but I hated it. I had to put a hook through this living thing, a worm, and it would writhe in pain in my hand. Then I'd put the hook in the water, and when a fish bit the worm, the hook would go in the fish's throat, almost tearing the fish's throat out. Then when I brought it up on the deck of the boat, the fish would be bleeding and flopping. I'd hit it, kill it, and eat it. This was fishing. One day, when my uncles were in the boat, I said to my father that I thought that was cruel. I was punished and told I was a sissy, and I was diminished by that experience. They were trying to prepare me for the cruelty of the real world by exercising a cruelty of their own.

One thing I realized from that experience was

that I did not want to be like that. These men were good human beings, but I wanted a definition of manhood that did not deny my horror at seeing two living creatures killed before my eyes. Boys who are allowed to feel and cry not only grow to have a regard for their own pain but are also sensitive to the pain of others.

During the sixties, through the drug revolution and the political revolution, assumptions were tossed into the air like a salad, and people were permitted to be who they were. I became a vegetarian for many years. I developed in the direction of accepting my body, my looks, and my mind, and the way I thought and felt about things. During that period of time, when I found out who I was as a human being, proving my manhood didn't really matter. In the final analysis, the only judgments that have any relevance are the judgments of God Almighty. ∎

"I used to have to go fishing, but I hated it."

—Bill Duke

Omar Tyree is an author, publisher, lecturer, and performance poet who has both literary talent and an entrepreneurial spirit. He self-published his first few novels, and their success captured the attention of a major publishing company. His entertaining string of African-American popular fiction includes *Flyy Girl, Single Mom,* and *For the Love of Money.*

Omar Tyree

seventeen years old, I got into a dispute over my gold chain. I let a girl wear it, but when I found out that she had a boyfriend, I took the necklace back from her. I was no sucker—I was not that kind of guy, and she was not going to play me. She told her boyfriend that I took the chain and roughed her up. He brought a whole crew of guys to my house looking for me. I thought, *I am not scared of the guy, but I'm not going outside, because I'm no damn fool.*

My father came home and wanted to know what all these cats were doing outside. I told him what happened, and my dad said, "Do you want to fight the boy?" I said, "I'm not afraid of him." So we went outside, where the guy and I got into a fight one-on-one.

I caught the boyfriend with a left hook and knocked him out. It was just like a boxing match, out in the middle of the street. His body hit the floor, and the fight was over. My pop called people saying, "He knocked him out with one punch," and the whole neighborhood knew. Men know what the heck that means. When I scored that knockout, the punch was about physical manhood.

The second phase of my manhood came when I started my own publishing company in October 1992. I was twenty-three years old and had just published my first book, *Colored on White Campus,* with my own money.

I sold the book myself, collected my own checks, made my own business deals, and represented myself. The books started to sell well. But my book *Flyy Girl* really made me a free man. Now I am talking about economic manhood.

The latest and strongest moment of my manhood was when my first son was born on May 31, 1996. I felt like I had gone to heaven when the doctor put my boy in my hands. This little dude looked like me, but he was better-looking and browner. He was muscular and handsome and didn't even have wrinkles.

As long as I am alive, I'm going to have more "manhood" points—maybe when my kids go to college or times when fatherhood is connected to manhood. But the physical and economic manhood and the family-father experience are the three points that have been the defining moments of manhood for me. ■

Taye Diggs

THE FIRST TIME I stood up to my father, as opposed to just standing by, was a turning point in my life. We lived in a very disciplined household in Rochester, New York. I was a junior or senior in high school and had just started to realize where the line was drawn between being my father's son and becoming my own man, standing up for what I believed was right. I don't know if I just felt that it was time, if it was a spiritual thing or my age, or if I'd just had enough, but I was feeling empowered. Suddenly I had the moxie, the guts, the courage to stand up for what I felt and not be frightened of what was to follow after expressing my opinion.

I'll never forget that day. My father said something, and I said he was wrong. This sticks in my mind because I have four brothers and sisters, and none of us had ever stood up to him, and I wasn't the type to cross anyone, least of all my father. He laughed at my challenge and accepted it. I didn't get a punch in the jaw, so I began to understand that it was cool to be myself.

Once you do something for the first time, no matter how difficult it is, it's much easier the second, third, and fourth time. After I had established the fact that I wasn't going to sit back any longer, I didn't need to step forward anymore. I think my father realized that I was a force to be reckoned with. I was too old to be spanked and old enough not to be frightened by anything he put forth. It was like we were on the same playing field. Our relationship began to transform and evolve. He respected me and started treating me more like an equal than a child. This was a coming-of-age experience for me. I was making the transition from boy to man. ■

Actor Taye Diggs achieved theatrical acclaim in 1996 for his role on Broadway in *Rent*. He then gained instant recognition for his feature film debut in *How Stella Got Her Groove Back*. This role led to further success in such films as *The Wood* and *The Best Man*. Diggs has also made his mark in featured television roles on *The Guiding Light* and *Ally McBeal*.

Neil deGrasse Tyson

IN 1991, I was one of seven Black astrophysicists in the country, out of what was then more than four thousand in the field. It was culturally lonely. When I attended society meetings of professional astrophysicists, there were essentially no Black people there.

I am also a member of the National Society of Black Physicists, an organization of Ph.D. research scientists in physics and related fields. Our meetings are held at historically Black colleges to inspire the next generation and encourage their participation in our conferences. Students don't necessarily understand everything we discuss and present, but they see, feel, taste, and touch an entire dimension of intellectual pursuit that they aren't privy to from watching television or going to the movies.

After a conference banquet near Jackson State College in Mississippi, a group of us—mostly Black men—grabbed our wine and went up to one of the common rooms in the hotel's penthouse. Late into the night, we discussed random

One of the leading astrophysicists in the nation, Dr. Neil deGrasse Tyson is the Frederick P. Rose Director of the Hayden Planetarium, part of the Rose Center for Earth and Space, the newest addition to the American Museum of Natural History. He is a member of the Museum's Department of Astrophysics and a visiting research scientist in the Department of Astrophysics at Princeton University. Since 1995, Tyson has written a monthly column for *Natural History* magazine. His research explores galaxies, star formation, and the galactic bulge of the Milky Way. His books include *The Sky Is Not the Limit: Adventures of an Urban Astrophysicist.*

scientific observations of the world around us. We talked about the accuracy of the police radar gun. The most moving dimension of that evening was when, triggered by this discussion of the radar guns, we took turns sharing our recollections of police encounters.

As we went around the room, every one of us told a story of being stopped by the police. The majority of our police stops were unwarranted, stemming from the offense of "Driving While Black." It required no effort to extrapolate what might have happened had circumstances been a little different. For all we knew, there might have been a physicist who wasn't at that meeting because he hadn't survived one of those encounters.

The irony was that we were Black men with the highest degrees in the land, and it didn't make a damn bit of difference. What we had in common went much deeper than our scientific backgrounds. Although we grew up as science kids with chemistry sets, telescopes, and microscopes, and we now fit the profile of scientists, in the end, through the lenses of society, we were just a roomful of "niggers."

Does the police harassment Black men endure happen to White men? At other scientific conferences, we retire to the common room, but my White colleagues don't talk much about the police. If one has a police story, it might be, "I was on spring break—drunk shit-faced—and the cop stopped me." I've thought, *What was I doing when the police stopped my car? I was totally sober, not speeding or in any way breaking the law.* I also wonder, *How much intellectual, emotional, and physical energy ends up diverted into the issue of racism?* Men in White America don't carry this burden. ■

" ...we were just a roomful of 'niggers.' "

—Neil deGrasse Tyson

Mumia Abu-Jamal

MANHOOD IS AN elastic concept that changes and develops over time. At a very young age, Black males learn, from their interaction with others, that something is amiss. The brilliant writer James Baldwin made just this point when he noted: "It comes as a great shock around the age of five, six, or seven to discover that the flag to which you have pledged allegiance, along with everybody else, had not pledged allegiance to you. It comes as a great shock to see Gary Cooper killing off the Indians and, although you are rooting for Gary Cooper, that the Indians are you."

For a young Black male, this is potent knowledge that defines you and marks your trajectory in life. From this foul seedling of knowledge can sprout the noxious weed of alienation or the blossom of belonging. One can emerge with the poison of aloneness, or the shared sense of commonality. As a fourteen-year-old, I joined the Black Panther Party (BPP) and became part of a revolutionary formation dedicated to defending the

Journalist and activist Mumia Abu-Jamal garnered national support following his controversial 1982 murder trial and conviction. Having spent almost two decades on death row, this outspoken critic of the American legal system has written three books, including *Live from Death Row* and *All Things Censored*.

Black community. I felt like a man. I joined the party about a year after another young man, Bobby Hutton, was murdered by Oakland cops, and like Bobby, I was fully prepared to give my life in defense of the party and our people's righteous struggle for freedom and self-determination. *Man,* then, meant militant defense, service, and sacrifice for one's people, one's community, and one's party.

Leaving the BPP, influenced by a deadly and fratricidal wave of party infighting that left young Panthers dead on both coasts, but occasioned by a love affair with a young Panther sister (and her resultant pregnancy), meant redefining my manhood. It meant becoming a committed

lover, companion, and father. And it meant the tortured mix of love and dread that marked the birth of a brown-skinned boy in this land—a feeling as perverse as it is terrible, a feeling as true as that two plus two equals four.

In the ultramacho world that is prison, manhood has many meanings, most involving the extent to which one can shield and mask feelings. No shield lasts forever. Slowly, almost imperceptibly, men who lost, or never had, fathers seek father figures among those elders whom they can trust—those who can teach them, who can give them a way to decode the maddening world that has been at war with them from birth, earn a trust that has rarely been given in a short, brutal life lived in cruel freedom. *Man,* in shackles, means griot, rememberer, teacher, decoder, and resister. Young men who have not bonded with their natural fathers and older men stripped from bonding with their natural sons develop new, if somewhat tenuous, bonds by creating shadows of family in the netherworld of prison.

So, *man* has various meanings, depending on the stage of one's life. It is he who defends, he who serves, he who sacrifices. ∎

Gerald Levert

WHEN MY MOM and dad divorced, I realized that I had to step up as the man of the house, to be there for my mother and help her through the hard times. I had so much love for my father; I felt so torn between the two of them. When a young man goes through something like this, it's a confusing mix of emotions. It can take you in many directions. You can start to hate your father. You're always going to love your mother because she's the caretaker and the nurturer, and because you've been taught to respect women. Seeing my mom cry really bothered me. Then seeing my father cry touched me and hurt my heart in another way. I became the referee, taking on the responsibility of keeping them from killing each other. All this drama and heartache taught me compassion and understanding.

It was the end of the 1980s, and my father was at a low point in his brilliant singing career. The O'Jays weren't making hits like they had back in the 1970s, and the pressure affected the whole family. My dad brought his tension home. We lived in a big mansion, with all kinds of stuff, and I was young and didn't understand why he would come home mad all the time.

During the 1970s, many acts didn't know how to handle their money properly—like paying taxes—and it caught up with them. This, too, was taking its toll on our family, and I felt I had to step up to the plate. I'm "Mr. Outspoken." I'm going to say what I feel. I had to get jobs and force my older and younger brothers, who were twenty-one and sixteen, to get jobs, too. On weekends we played in clubs. I was singing, but I knew that my father was frustrated because he wasn't.

I felt like I had to bring everything back together. I was somewhat able to do that. My brothers and I formed a singing group, Levert, and managed to get a record deal, which resulted in a number one record. I started producing my dad, and we started touring. We were able to make money together, and we haven't looked back since.

In retrospect, all of this—my parents' divorce, my stepping up to the plate and doing what I could to help my family—has made me the man I am. It made me much harder than I would've been, but in the music business you have to be that way. You have to be strong. ■

Gerald Levert has proven his talents as a songwriter, vocalist, and producer by selling 10 million albums since first emerging in the 1980s. He formed the singing trio Levert in 1985, a collaboration that resulted in six gold albums. The son of Eddie Levert of the legendary O'Jays, Gerald went on to pursue a successful solo career that has earned both gold and platinum albums.

Derrick Bell

Derrick Bell is a
compelling voice on
issues of race and class
in this society.
Throughout his forty-year
career as a lawyer,
activist, teacher, and
writer, he has provoked
his critics and
challenged his readers
with his uncompromising
candor and original,
progressive views. Bell
became the first tenured
Black professor at
Harvard Law School in
1971, a position he
relinquished in 1992 as
a personal protest
against the lack of
women of color on the
faculty. He became a
visiting professor at
New York University
Law School. His many
published works include
four books featuring
Geneva Crenshaw. One
of his stories, "Space
Traders," was produced
as an HBO movie.

I HAD KNOWN powerful and brave women from my many years as a civil rights lawyer in the South, but like so many of my contemporaries, I did not make the connection between racism and sexism. For a long time I thought race and sex were separate agendas, but I slowly came around to agreeing with my women students—White as well as Black—who had been telling me for years that we Blacks must deal with sexism and patriarchy in our communities before we can effectively address the continuing evils of racism.

Indeed, the character Geneva Crenshaw has been both my fictional alter ego and my seer. She has been my surrogate in my quest to do justice to the dreams and aspirations of my students as I sought greater understanding of the civil rights struggles in which I had been engaged. I thought—probably with more than a little arrogance—that litigating dozens of lawsuits to break the back of racism in the Deep South had either given me dispensation from other sins or made me immune to them. The teaching experience, and my students, opened my eyes and my heart.

I came to understand that, like Whites who want Blacks to stay "in their place," Black men who want women to be subordinate are causing alienation and human suffering. Whites may not think that they have to change; we can't afford not to. Black men must absolutely abstain from acting on our society's sexist and patriarchal assumptions and doing things that demean women. We need to build a nation within a nation.

Acknowledging Black-male patriarchy is not to burden Black men with more recrimination. This society has not much loved either Black men or Black women, and debate about whether society's hostility or Black-male rage directed on itself has done more harm doesn't move us closer to the relief we need. Our relief must come through defining and building strengths within ourselves. This is an issue of equity and survival. ■

Omar Wasow

Internet analyst and commentator Omar Wasow has been called a "pioneer in Silicon Alley" for having the foresight to create New York Online during the early days of the Internet. As the executive director of BlackPlanet.com, he helped the site become one of the fastest-growing Internet communities on the Web. He provides analysis and commentary for MSNBC and NBC's New York affiliate, as well as for *USA Today.* A Stanford graduate with a degree in Race and Ethnic Relations, Wasow has worked on voter registration and a program for ex–drug dealers. Wasow was selected as a Rockefeller Foundation Fellow in the Next Generation Leadership Program.

WHEN ATTENDING A jazz performance at New York City's Lincoln Center, I was really struck by the way the brothers onstage carried themselves. There was clearly a style, a rhythm, and an aesthetic that was not simply about a love of jazz. It was beyond the music; it was about the dignity of the Black man. Sadly, this is a value that seems to be missing in my generation. Having a sense of protocol and grace about what you do has become a lost art. Many young brothers have not been exposed to these images; they don't know that there is a way you can be a gentleman—be gentle, and be a man.

The media must accept their share of the blame for contributing to the demise of Black manhood. The Black man is portrayed as the ultimate gangster in movies and hip-hop culture, although that's not how most Black men live. Art is about freedom, and in that context these portrayals are fine, but when those images and behavior begin to define Black-male identity, they are not. Ultimately, the celebration of "gangsterism," or as KRS-One says, being "criminal-minded," has crept up on us as an enormous segment of the economy in our communities has become illegal. If I became king tomorrow and could wave a magic wand, I would dramatically change the landscape for young Black men. If drugs were decriminalized, I think that you would see the dissolution of that criminal class that has gained too strong a foothold in our communities.

The war on drugs has been enormously destructive for Black men. Over the last twenty to twenty-five years, it has produced a Black gangster class that has been celebrated and that has corrupted many of the core values in our community. That celebration of this lifestyle has been misplaced, because these brothers, too, are suffering and languishing in prisons throughout the nation.

I believe that by decriminalizing drugs, you alleviate the reason that so many of our brothers are being held in jails for drug-related offenses. For proof of that, just look at the history of the prohibition of alcohol, which led to a gangster class and unprecedented levels of violence. With the repeal of prohibition, you saw declines in murder rates and gangsterism.

Once upon a time, the people we most admired were the most upstanding. Hard-working people who earned an honest living were the pillars in the community.

But there's been a major shift in our values. Today the people who are most admired are the people who are getting paid—no matter how they earn the money. The war on drugs is a very powerful and pernicious force that has had the effect of criminalizing too many Black men. In the process, we have lost our sense of grace and honor. Dignity and eloquence captivated the Lincoln Center audience who had gathered to hear some young jazz musicians play. Reclaiming that posture of elegant dignity is our monumental challenge. ■

"If drugs were decriminalized, I think that you would see the dissolution of that criminal class . . . in our communities."

—Omar Wasow

E. Lynn Harris

THERE WERE TWO points in my life when I was challenged to take on what I view as responsibilities of manhood. The first was at thirteen, when my mom got divorced from my abusive stepfather. Suddenly I felt responsible not only for my mother, but for my sisters as well, because I was the oldest. I started to work, since my mom was working three jobs while trying to raise us. Looking back, I see how courageous she was to end a relationship that was bad for her *and* for the whole family.

I was challenged again when I started writing, because I had to tell the truth about myself. When I began to write, I tried to separate myself from the work by saying, "*Invisible Life* is a book. It isn't about me, it's a novel." But when I started to get letters from people telling me how much the book meant to them and how deeply they were touched by it, I realized how important it was for me to tell the truth. A big part of being a man is being honest with yourself, facing who you are, and being at peace with that.

There are many gay and bisexual men who deny that truth. They lie about who they are, and hurt themselves and others. If a woman falls in love with a man pretending to be somebody else—anybody else—that pretender is not being a responsible man; he's not assuming an important responsibility of manhood, which is being honorable.

When I left home at eighteen to study at the University of Arkansas, my mom and sisters were so proud because I was doing something no one else in our family had done: I was going to college. There I found myself alone for the first time, and in my loneliness and confusion I created a make-believe existence. I'd been awarded several scholarships and grants, so I had money and pretended to be from a wealthy family. I lived like a rich kid. Amazingly, my mom had saved money because she expected me to go to college. When I got the scholarships and grants, she bought me a car. Once I left home, I got caught up in the world. I wasn't a

responsible man or the man my mother had raised me to be.

When I was a boy, I thought I had to be a tough guy. I thought I had to play sports. But I was a small kid, and I couldn't do the sports thing very well, so I became the class clown. If I made people laugh, I thought, maybe they would like me, wouldn't notice how small I was and that I had effeminate traits. I was always focused on appearing "manly," acting like a tough guy, concentrating on not doing things like crossing my legs. Later when I went to work for IBM, I adopted a strict business image. I wore only blue suits and white shirts and did what I thought was necessary to succeed in the corporate world—including having girlfriends.

You see, when you're different—when you're gay or bisexual—you feel like you often let people down. And it's easy to feel you're not a man, because you're not procreating. But despite the pressures of society, I've come to love and accept myself as a man. I've reached a point where I have the respect of my peers and the love of my friends, most of whom are women. And I am a man who has made my mother proud. ■

Alvin Poussaint

I BECAME AWARE early on that as a Black man I was going to be discriminated against. At age ten, I became very sick with rheumatic fever. I was sent to a convalescence home and the kids called me a "Black booger" and a "nigger," so I went to the head nurse, crying. "They keep calling me a nigger." She looked me dead straight in the eyes and said, "Well, ain't you a nigger?"

This was Far Rockaway, New York, in about 1944. Even though today I am a psychiatrist, I cannot erase that experience from my memory. It traumatized me in a very deep way. I was looking for this nurse, someone I held in high esteem, to rescue me and say that this "nigger" stuff was something that kids just did and that it wouldn't be tolerated. That was my first encounter with racism. It dawned on me how White people thought.

When I was a teenager in East Harlem, there were always brushes with the police, but this one I'll never forget: I was about fifteen, walking one of my sister's White girlfriends home from school through Central Park. The police grabbed me and separated us, told me to go stand by the tree, started asking her what she was doing with a nigger, and actually said they would escort her to the subway. One of the policemen came over to me, and I thought he was going to beat my brains out, but he said, "I bet you're coming in your pants already." I was confused, thinking, *What is this all about?* I began to understand the depths of racism and the fear among White men around issues involving White women and Black men. It really frightened me.

In elementary school we had a song, "Round, Round, Nigger Baby," which the kids sang and did a dance to. In junior high school, we sang "Without a Song," which includes the lyrics "A

darkie's born, but he's no good without a song." I'd play the clarinet, and they would give us sheet music of "Old Man River," which started, "Nigger-folks work on the Mississippi, nigger-folks work . . ."

I became very aware that Black men—that Black people—were despised in many sectors of society. It made me struggle with serious feelings of inferiority and self-doubt, and the only thing that kept me going, frequently, was just saying I wasn't going to quit. If I was going to flunk out, I was going to go down fighting. But still, there was self-doubt.

As I moved on through college and medical school, I would see that segregated medicine meant that society didn't value a Black life as much as a White life, and that racism permeated all the nation's systems and institutions. In any area of medicine, Blacks are not being served in the same way as Whites, whether it's getting evaluated properly or having equal access to bypass surgery, getting equal access to pain medication, or being referred to the best surgeons versus being referred to surgeons in training. I continue to challenge those intrinsic views that permeate a two-tier medical system.

Some years ago, while working in the South during the Civil Rights Movement, I witnessed segregated medicine in a graphic, raw form. Black patients were in dirty wards, with broken-down beds and broken equipment. It was not just disenfranchisement of Blacks, but the devaluation of Black life. This exemplified what institutional racism is: inequity. In segregated medicine, there is a willingness to let Black people die rather than healing them, a willingness to let Black women have babies in pickup trucks outside the hospital. I saw all of that, and it had a profound effect on me and on my understanding of the depths of racism, and how difficult it was going to be to eradicate it.

And I'm still struggling. The White community still doesn't understand the pain we feel when we see that Confederate flag hanging above government buildings—what it does to us psychologically. It causes us pain. But they don't understand.

I am challenging the American Psychiatric Association to look at racism as a mental disorder, which they refuse to do. When people start shooting Blacks and Jews because of race and religion, they are deranged. Why isn't psychiatry looking at this, trying to understand it? Why can't you find in the index of their diagnostic manual the words "racism" or "prejudice"?

We have to stay strong and keep fighting, because the world is being interpreted from a White perspective, which is frequently flawed and often mingled with racism. ∎

Alvin Poussaint, M.D., began his distinguished medical career during the height of the civil rights struggle as the South Field Director of the Medical Committee for Human Rights in Mississippi, providing medical care to civil rights workers and aiding in the desegregation of health facilities. He went on to join the faculty of Tufts Medical School and later Harvard Medical School, where he has been director of the media center in the Judge Baker Children's Center, a clinical professor of psychiatry, and faculty associate dean for student affairs.

St. Clair Bourne

BECOMING AN ADULT means exploring and defining what you think life is and how you fit into it. It is important to figure out what you want to do, not only in terms of a job, but also in terms of what you want to achieve, and how important money, position, and power are to you. All of this is important for self-definition. But no matter what your calling is, you should practice and nourish sensitivity to others. Without sensitivity, we become chauvinistic, focusing only on what *we* want. Through sensitivity to others, we become complete human beings.

I'm a filmmaker, and what has amazed me about most of the people I've documented in my forty films is their self-awareness and fierce ambition. Even more amazing—and instructive—has been their deep sense of caring and sensitivity toward others. As an artist, I search for truth, and I've found that often these great people also seek truth, even if it's only the truth about themselves.

I went to college at Georgetown University Foreign Service School, an all-White and really corny environment, but nearby was Black D.C. and Howard University, where I socialized. Like most young men, I was always trying to get over with the sisters, but I'll never forget what one woman taught me. I thought I had seduced her, but in the afterglow, she turned to me and said, "I hope you won't hurt me." Clearly, she had been hurt before, and to me that was a plea not to wound her again. I remember thinking, *You can't try to get down with every woman just for your own self-satisfaction*. It had never occurred to me that life wasn't all about getting what you want, but that day, what has become a guiding force in my life kicked in—you've got to be responsible.

That's when I began to grow up, to become a man. Trying to live righteously as a human being and not to hurt others in the pursuit of something you want is to live fully, to be complete. ■

Independent filmmaker St. Clair Bourne has produced a body of exceptional work that remains faithful to his politically based aesthetic, often celebrating the historical figures and events of our time. As the head of his production company, Chamba Mediaworks, producer, director, and writer Bourne has made more than forty films. Among his accomplishments are directing *Paul Robeson: Here I Stand* for PBS and coproducing a documentary about photojournalist and filmmaker Gordon Parks for HBO.

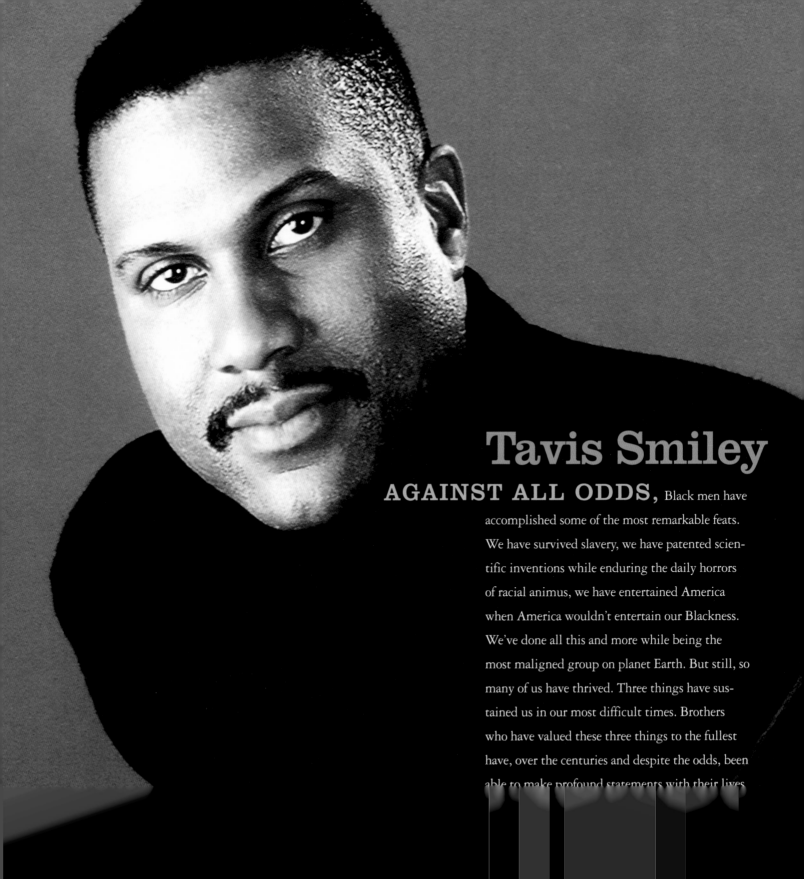

Tavis Smiley

AGAINST ALL ODDS, Black men have accomplished some of the most remarkable feats. We have survived slavery, we have patented scientific inventions while enduring the daily horrors of racial animus, we have entertained America when America wouldn't entertain our Blackness. We've done all this and more while being the most maligned group on planet Earth. But still, so many of us have thrived. Three things have sustained us in our most difficult times. Brothers who have valued these three things to the fullest have, over the centuries and despite the odds, been able to make profound statements with their lives.

Faith is number one. The Bible says that "faith is the substance of things hoped for, the evidence of things not seen." Seldom can Black men look down the road and see anything positive about to happen. For Black men, faith in God has been a sustaining factor—having faith to move forward without a reason to believe, but believing anyway and knowing that all life's challenges work out in the end.

Family is second. We don't appreciate family as we should. Life is so much more rewarding when you have people around you to share your successes and your challenges. Having nine brothers and sisters I learned the value of having people who will stand with you when everybody else is against you. Every Black man should know what it is to be loved in an unconditional way. We're not always loved unconditionally in romantic relationships. Your boss certainly won't love you unconditionally. Often friends won't. But a loving family will not fail you.

Third and last are friendships. As Black men, many of us have not cultivated friendships with Black women. We see them as sex objects, so we don't nourish and nurture friendships with sisters. My mother taught me a long time ago that if you want something done right, you'd better be sure a woman's got your back. I learned that lesson well. I have five women on my immediate team, and I don't mean secretaries, but sisters who run my entire operation, from my newsletter to my Web site. It's about appreciating Black women for the intellect, joy, stability, and discipline they bring to our lives, and appreciating them as friends. It's the brothers who have strong ties with sisters—in relationships, friendships, and businesses—who go farthest.

We also have to maintain solid friendships with other Black men. So much of the "playa-hatin' " that we see every day—whether it's Bloods against Crips, the alleged East Coast–West Coast rap conflict, or brothers killing each other in the streets—has got to stop. With the high rate of Black-on-Black crime in our communities, we are more challenged than ever to support and lock arms with one another. When a Black man kills a White man, he gets the death penalty—and quickly. When a White man kills a Black man, we either want to march in the streets or loot and burn the city. But when a Black man kills another Black man, nobody sees, hears, or knows anything. There is but one way to stop Black nihilism—to love each and every Black man as we love ourselves.

Brothers who have developed strong faith, family, and friends in their lives are the Black men we admire most. When you fulfill these areas of your life in a meaningful way, people take note and feel inspired. ■

As the host of his own show, Tavis Smiley has interviewed some of the most fascinating and significant newsmakers of our time, including President Bill Clinton, Fidel Castro, Pope John Paul II, and Prince. Smiley, who was an aide to former Los Angeles mayor Tom Bradley, is also a political commentator and analyst on the *Tom Joyner Morning Show* and CNN. He is the author of two books and the publisher of his own newsletter, *The Smiley Report.*

PASSION

The magic of the day is the morning
I want to say the day is morning high
and sweet, good
morning.
The ballad of the morning streets, sweet
voices turns
of cool warm weather
high around the early windows grey to blue
and down again amongst the kids and
broken sighs, is pure love magic, sweet day
come into me, let me live with you
and dig your blazing

—Amiri Baraka

DMX

Since his explosive
debut in 1998, Earl
Simmons, better known
as DMX, has held the
hip-hop world spellbound
with his raw, unbridled
energy. DMX was the
first artist to have two
number-one albums and
a successful film, *Belly*,
in the same year. Having
a special place in his
heart for children, DMX
contributes to pediatric
AIDS causes and
sponsors a summer
camp for kids with AIDS.

FOR MOST OF my life, I have been surrounded by loneliness, pain, and death. I know what it is to lose a loved one—whether through abandonment, separation, or death. So as a youngster I befriended dogs, and I learned an important lesson about life and love. When I refer to dog love, I'm talking about the way a dog loves its master unconditionally—despite all of his faults, flaws, and failures. I have always wondered why it is so difficult for human beings to do the same.

I've never changed—I'm the kid who parents told their kids to stay away from. Strangely, now that I am at the top of the charts, everyone says how much they love me. But let's keep it real. The only one who loved me then and who loves me now is God. That is why it is so important for me to acknowledge Him on all of my albums.

The defining moments of my life were the births of my sons. For the first time, I was truly responsible for life. To hold my sons in my arms and know they love me is a feeling I would not trade for anything else in the world. I have the chance to be everything that I wanted my father to be. While my sons may find my accomplishments impressive, their love for me transcends the awards and record sales. They love "Daddy" unconditionally. In fact, they are a reflection of God's love for me. And that to me is truly the definition of life—to know God, for God is love. ■

Wynton Marsalis

Wynton Marsalis is one of the most accomplished and celebrated musicians of his era, with an unmatched creative output on both the jazz and classical music scenes. He has earned more than eight Grammy Awards for his recordings. As the artistic director of New York's Jazz at Lincoln Center, Marsalis is internationally recognized, and through his Lincoln Center Jazz for Young People series, he devotes countless hours to supporting music education. Marsalis is the first jazz musician to win a Pulitzer Prize, and his artistry extends to composing for dance. He has received numerous honors for his extraordinary talent.

IF I COULD give one gift to young brothers, I would give them the gift of healing. Our young brothers need to be healed. I'm not just talking about the poor ones you see all the time in the news, the stereotypical image portrayed in the media: young men in the inner cities who come from broken families, who have a pile of gold in their mouths and a perpetual scowl, and show their asses all the time. Although there are many types of brothers, I always see the one-dimensional images of us killing each other and tearing down our communities. Our young Black men need to be healed of the negative images that can be so ingrained in our psyches that our self-esteem is destroyed. We start to believe and to act like what we see, not realizing that everyone has the power to create. Why create yourself as a fool or be duped into believing you can't compete on a real level without losing your roots?

That's why I'd give the gift of healing. The healer might just put a hand on a troubled brother's shoulder, look him in the eye and say, "Man, it's all right." A word of truth can help things become all right. A healer might give a brother who's trying to do something positive in the community the fortitude to raise the money to build a center, or go to a young man's house and teach him how to cook a good meal. He might give him advice on how to deal with the death of a family member or the breakup of a relationship. He could be someone who teaches a brother how to take care of his kids properly.

A person who wants to help us become well is a healer. It may be a television producer who says, "Man, let's stop putting negative images of brothers in our programs." Or a record company executive who says, "I'm going to be the one to stop putting all these ignorant lyrics and negative aspirations out there, even though they are making me rich." That one act can be compared to that of the first slave trader who said, "I'm making a pile of money, but I won't trade slaves anymore." It's hard to turn your back on money. But it isn't hard for a healer—a person focused on uplifting, not exploiting, people. ∎

Jim Brown

I AM A human being in the eyes of God, but my passion and my political beliefs define who I am as a Black man. I was born into a society where Black people were discriminated against and racist attitudes were prevalent. Each day of my life, I wondered what was going to come at me next from the dominant race. My manhood was tied up in fighting against second-class citizenship and racist attitudes. That led me into bonding with Black men in general, but also in specific ways. It led me to connect with those who shared my passion about fighting discrimination and racism.

Two men whom I've called close brothers and with whom I have shared common experiences were Malcolm X and Huey P. Newton. I bonded with Malcolm X when I was in Miami as a football player during the time of Muhammad Ali's fight with Sonny Liston. Malcolm and Muhammad Ali had been friends for some time, and Malcolm was there to solicit Muhammad Ali to join him in the new organization he had formed after leaving the Nation

of Islam. Each day Malcolm and I used to talk. Because he had been suspended from the Nation of Islam, he wasn't popular, and many people were afraid to be in his company. He'd made some controversial comments about Elijah Muhammad and the late President Kennedy and had almost become an outcast. But I welcomed him because he was one Black man who spoke out against racism in a manner I thought was appropriate. Instead of being apologetic, he was definitely ready to lay out the facts about racism.

Then there was my relationship with Huey P. Newton—a revolutionary with a brilliant mind. During some of his troubled times, he and I would get together at my home or go to the house of a Hollywood producer who worked with the Panthers. I was always very proud of our friendship because I knew he was very passionate about the work the Panthers had done.

In the sixties, lots of Black brothers had a passion for justice that we demonstrated in different ways. Even though I didn't march with Martin

Football legend and activist Jim Brown built upon a record-setting career as the premier fullback for the Cleveland Browns in the late 1950s and mid-1960s to become a notable Hollywood actor appearing in more than twenty films. But he takes great pride in his work to help empower the disenfranchised—from people challenged by the correctional system to at-risk young adults. He is the founder and the president of the Amer-I-Can Program, a national program that teaches participants self-determination and responsibility.

Luther King, Jr., I understood his passion. I knew it was real, though I didn't believe in marching, singing, and praying. The Panthers had guns, but I didn't believe in guns either. I believed in economic development. I had great respect for the people fighting diligently in both camps—all of them—and we were all fighting for the same things. We wanted freedom, we wanted our constitutional rights, and we wanted to be included.

Today I don't find that same passion in many of our high-profile brothers. Back in the sixties, Sidney Poitier, Harry Belafonte, Bill Russell, and other athletes and entertainers were always right in the midst of the poor people, fighting alongside them. Now I find that we have developed an elite group of entertainers and athletes who make tremendous amounts of money and have great commercial value, but they lack passion for the freedom of all our people.

For the first time in modern history, we have a very serious dividing line between the poor and disenfranchised and the rich and enfranchised. Out of that divide comes gang violence, Black-on-Black crime, and a lack of self-esteem among young, poor Black men around this country. I'm passionate about doing something about that. ■

"My manhood was tied up in fighting against second-class citizenship and racist attitudes."
—Jim Brown

John Edgar Wideman

MY PASSIONS COME and go, changing over time. I've been passionate about writing for most of my life. And basketball has, at times, been equally important.

With basketball I can lie a lot. I can say, "I was the greatest. I don't remember the last time I missed a shot. I was a great jumper and good on defense." If the truth be told, I simply loved the game. It was my way of relaxing, so the pressure on the court never seemed very intense. It didn't weigh down on me the way other kinds of pressure did. As a kid, it was a way of proving myself among the guys.

Once I started playing organized ball, it was that much-sought-after equal playing field, where, as a young African-American man, I

Author and English professor John Edgar Wideman has written more than a dozen novels, as well as short fiction, critical articles, and essays. In 1984, he won the prestigious PEN/Faulkner Award for *Sent for You Yesterday,* the third book in his Homewood Trilogy, which describes his Pittsburgh community. He received the award a second time in 1991 for *Philadelphia Fire.* A 1963 Rhodes scholar, Wideman was a star athlete and brilliant scholar while in college. Since then, he has received numerous honors for his literary prowess and professional accomplishments.

could be a winner if I was good enough. If I worked hard and brought discipline and skills to the game, I had a chance to be the best on any given day. That was a unique situation. I figured out pretty early that basketball was my ticket to school—through sports and scholarships. But that was secondary, only in the back of my mind. Ultimately, I simply loved the game.

I had a bifurcated childhood. Part of the time I lived in Homewood, which was an 80 percent Black neighborhood in Pittsburgh, and part of the time I lived in an area called Shadyside, which was more middle-class and had only one or two streets where Black people lived. Homewood was the basketball turf. There were many more players, and there was a great playground where professionals and college guys played, so that was part of my basketball education. Shadyside was dull, with only one basket on a dirt softball field. I was always much better than the kids in Shadyside because of that

grounding in Homewood. I continued to play ball through high school, college, and semipro. Bill Bradley and I met through basketball and began a lifelong friendship playing against each other when he was at Princeton and I was at Penn, before we played together later at Oxford.

Many aspects of my life have revolved around basketball. One of the saddest, hardest things I've ever had to do was to give it up because of age and obsolescence. In a way, it's a young man's game, and if you can't let it all hang out, then it takes some of the fun away. Because it's such a special game, there are old-timers who play all over the country. In any big city on Saturday or Sunday mornings you'll find a group of mainly African-American men wrapping their knees, trash-talking, and playing the game. If you play with your peers, you can go on forever—almost. If they get old, you grow old with them. You play a slower version, and it's all still fun. ■

Charlie Ward

Following a Heisman Trophy–winning football career as quarterback at Florida State University, Charlie Ward chose a career in professional basketball over football in 1994, when he was selected in the first round by the New York Knicks. He has won acclaim as one of the best backup point guards in the NBA. Ward has also dedicated hundreds of hours to community service and charitable organizations. He is a member of Big Brothers/Big Sisters and spends quality time with his little brother every week.

BEING AN ATHLETE gives me a platform from which to share the word of God. The biggest challenge is publicly acknowledging the source of our gifts and talents and not being embarrassed or worried about what other people think. There are a lot of distractions on the road. That was one of the reasons I wanted a ministry where Christian athletes in the NBA could come together.

The 1999 CAUSE (Christian Athletes United for Spiritual Empowerment) Summit was very powerful because God was really doing something in my life. I also had an opportunity to be in the presence of Bishop T. D. Jakes and Pastor Miles Monroe. Brother Reggie White was there, as well as Cris Carter, Randall Cunningham, Keith Jackson, and many other football and basketball players. There was a great opportunity to enjoy fellowship with them and gain a sense of what God is doing in their lives. CAUSE was born out of the need for Christian athletes to minister to other athletes.

That summit was the first time that I had ever been in the spirit, and it was very out of character for me. I saw that anything can happen when you're dealing with the power of God. It took me to another level along my Christian walk in faith—to the point where I'm now not afraid of anything. It took me three or four years to get to this point, but that's the way God works.

When I started studying the word of God, I had to change my outlook and lifestyle. I started listening to different types of music and stopped my college habits of engaging in premarital sex and watching pornography, which had led to my exploiting women. I realize now that these are things that go along with the cycle of seeing—that God had to change my life in order for me to become the best husband, teammate, and friend that I could be. All the things that people didn't know about me were eating me up inside. God had to change me, and it was hard, but I got on my knees and asked for forgiveness of my sins.

Although I gave my life to Christ when I was about ten, it's been an uphill journey ever since. I haven't been an angel, and I'm sure no one else has, but I know the greatness of God. He has given us grace. ◼

David Satcher

As the second person in U.S. history to hold simultaneously the positions of surgeon general and assistant secretary for health, David Satcher, M.D., has dedicated his life to making effective public-health programs available to all Americans. He directed the King-Drew Sickle Cell Research Center for six years and is a former faculty member of the UCLA School of Medicine and Public Health. Dr. Satcher has also served as president of Meharry Medical School and professor and chairman of the Department of Community Medicine and Family Practice at the Morehouse School of Medicine.

WHEN I WAS two years old, I came down with whooping cough, which is an upper-respiratory infection accompanied by a rhythmic cough and difficulty breathing. In my case, it turned into pneumonia and a very high fever. Many people were sick back in the 1940s from a vast variety of ailments, and my parents had lost a child a year before. My condition was very serious.

Back then Blacks weren't allowed to go to the hospital in Anniston, Alabama. But my dad was able to get Dr. Jackson, the only Black physician in our area, to come to our farm. Dr. Jackson spent the whole day working with me, trying to control my fever and clear my chest. Despite the doctor's efforts, I didn't seem to be improving. He told my parents that he had done everything he could do and that they shouldn't expect me to live through the week. But he took the time to show my mother how to control my fever and keep my chest clear. She did that, and I survived.

My parents were Christians and people of great faith. They felt very strongly that their prayers, and the prayers of the people who were holding vigils on our porch during that time, made a difference in my recovery. Afterward, my mother never let me forget what happened. Almost every day she told me that story, and I became extremely curious about Dr. Jackson and wanted to meet him. My father would say, "When you're five years old, I'm going to take you to town to meet the doctor." Dr. Jackson died the year before my fifth birthday, but even though I never met him, he inspired me.

By age six, I told everyone that I was going to be a doctor. I don't think anyone took me seriously, because nobody in our house had been to college or even finished high school. But I dreamed of making the kind of difference in people's lives that Dr. Jackson had made in mine. I saw myself as having a purpose that was bigger than me, and that vision became my driving force.

My vision compelled me to take twenty-mile bus rides to segregated schools when the White school was only a mile away. It took me through years of working odd jobs as a patrol boy, in the foundries while in high school, and at Jeff's Barbecue. It took me to jail during civil rights protests. That vision of becoming a doctor helped me through life's adversities. I knew if I held on to it, I'd make it—and I did. ■

James Alexander Forbes, Jr.

Appointed in 1989 as the first African-American to serve as senior minister at New York City's landmark Riverside Church, the Reverend Dr. James Alexander Forbes, Jr., is known for his impassioned messages and charismatic style. Before being called to Riverside's pulpit, Dr. Forbes taught preaching at Union Theological Seminary in New York City and held pastorates at several other churches. He is an ordained minister in the American Baptist Churches and the Original United Holy Church of America.

WHEN I ACCEPTED my call to become a Christian minister, I was a chemistry major at Howard University, and I had every intention of going on to medical school. But before the end of my junior year, I felt a deep urge to give up the prospect of a medical career and take up healing on a broader scale, through ministry.

It wasn't an easy decision to make, because I dreaded the idea of being a minister. You don't make as much money as in medicine, and people are always trying to run your life. But even in the midst of my indecision, I had a sense that the ministry was what God wanted me to do.

One night after praying and asking God for direction, I was led to Psalm 27: "The Lord is my light and my salvation, whom shall I fear? The Lord is the strength of my life, of whom shall I be afraid?" That was my epiphany. I put aside my plans for medical school and prepared to go directly to seminary instead. In the late 1950s, I applied to the theological program at Duke University, but they wrote me back saying they did not accept Negro students and didn't intend to do so in the foreseeable future. I was disappointed but not deterred. I taught science for one year and later matriculated at Union Theological Seminary in New York.

Over the years, during times of uncertainty, I have been able to reflect on that moment of discovery and be assured that, yes, the vocation I was pursuing was the one to which God had called me. I also knew that, yes, God would provide me with everything I needed to be faithful to that call, and that my satisfaction in life would come as I fulfilled my responsibility as a Christian minister. I have no regrets, only deep satisfaction that I was considered worthy to be a part of the ministry. ■

Blair Underwood

"TO LOVE ANOTHER person is to see the face of God. And I know when your hair turns silver and our faces are weathered with age that I will see God shining through your eyes, as I do now." When I was married in California on September 17, 1994, these are the words I said to my bride.

We had gotten engaged at the foot of the Eiffel Tower in Paris on New Year's Eve the year before, so our wedding cake was a six-foot-tall replica of the Eiffel Tower. All six of my groomsmen and I rode in on horseback over a hillside—we had eleven horses in the wedding. We partied into the night.

About four months later my wife, Désirée, and I went to South Africa on another honeymoon. We were there for two weeks, and we made many new friends. The day before we were to leave for home, our friends convinced us to go to one more party. We were exhausted, but we went anyway. When we arrived, our host announced, "I know you got married in America, but now that you've come home to the Motherland, we want to throw you a traditional African wedding." A surprise wedding!

They took us into different rooms and dressed us in South African attire. Our friends in America had told us that we were not to assume we had come home unless the folks there embraced us in that way. So it was extraordinary for our African friends to have gone to all that trouble to give us this wonderful ceremony. Désirée and I felt so full. To receive that emotion and love from the men and women in South Africa filled a void we had never realized existed. And we know that the memories of our South African wedding will be with us throughout our long life together. ■

Actor Blair Underwood attained fame for his portrayal of a confident, passionate lawyer on the NBC series *L.A. Law.* He has since earned acclaim for notable television dramas, including *City of Angels.* Underwood's impressive credits include such films as *Deep Impact* and *Rules of Engagement,* as well as theater acting, producing, and directing. In 1980, Underwood cofounded Artists for a New South Africa, which supports equal rights and opportunities for South Africans.

Chinua Achebe

Internationally known author Chinua Achebe, a native of Nigeria, has written novels, short stories, essays, and poetry. His most celebrated works include *Things Fall Apart, A Man of the People,* and *Anthills of the Savannah.* As a professor of English, he has taught at the University of Nigeria, the University of Massachusetts at Amherst, the University of Connecticut, and Bard College, where he became Charles Stevenson Professor of Languages and Literature in 1990.

THE STORY I told in my book *Things Fall Apart* is that of an African people. But if you look deeper, I'm really talking about Black people in general. This book is about a people living their lives—and then thrown into disarray by foreign invaders.

The world is full of people whose stories have not been told. And I belong to that group. I recognized quite early in my life that my story was not among the works that I read about or that people spoke about. What was even worse was that a counterfeit tale had been put forward as my story. My mission has been to rediscover the true story and tell it.

When Europe first encountered Africa during Europe's so-called Age of Discovery in the late fifteenth and early sixteenth centuries, Africa had diverse political institutions—from small-scale communities to large empires. Everywhere you looked you could find new political entities developing just like those that were in Europe. But with the coming of the Europeans, the development in Africa stopped. The moment the slave trade gathered full momentum, Africa began to pay a terrible price for Europe's visit—hundreds of years of slavery followed by colonial occupation. We became a people who no longer knew their story.

Rediscovering our history has been a long and difficult but very rewarding adventure. It's not something that I could finish in one book, two books, or even one hundred books. We need thousands of books to deny the lies. The work is only beginning, not just for Black people, but for everyone whose stories and humanity have been denied. One of the most rewarding experiences to come from my writing is the number of people I know in my town, my country, and ultimately throughout Africa who say to me, "This is our story. I'd nearly forgotten. Thank you." ■

THE ARTS

I investigate
the sun. Let it do me when it come.
I fancy myself Pythagoras sometimes. I find
out what its fire and brightness mean. For
the old lady polishing floors up on the hill
for the permanently smiling, I support her
music, as it trembles against that dazzling
flo. I resist bald head guys with pointed teeth
and white collars pulled outside they coats
suppose to be powerful. My rejoinder and
answer, my constant line they all grow hard
against, where are you in the sun's shine,
what you know of its fire? Have you checked
your vain insistence against life's life, yellow
& read & atomic before atomic, how does

your projection list against Ra's ra ra? No,
for real, I investigate the sun. I am paid for
this vocation, it's not above my station, sun
checker for a nation, magnifying glass for a
class, I investigate the sun. Bring back its
dance and music, its design and hip rime.
Sun poet Sun singer warrior Sun why you
what you who you have you those my
questions as I rise into
its hot glamour. I investigate the sun.
Doubt it if you will, what
does a shadow know anyway?
I investigate the sun.

—Amiri Baraka

John Singleton

When John Singleton
made his directorial
debut with the coming-
of-age film *Boyz N the
Hood,* he held the
distinction of being the
youngest person and the
first African-American to
be nominated for an
Academy Award as Best
Director. Singleton has
gone on to direct many
films, including *Poetic
Justice, Higher Learning,
Rosewood, Shaft 2000,*
and *Baby Boy.*

THE MOST SIGNIFICANT events in my life have occurred in and around movie theaters. My father used to take me to films all the time. He's one of those Black folks who, if he enjoys himself, you know it. He laughs, talks, and screams loud.

When I was nine years old my father took me to see *The Island of Dr. Moreau.* Watching the film, my dad was laughing really loud and having a good time. A White cat in front of us turned around and said, "Could you keep it down; could you just speak a little bit more softly?" My father kicked his chair and said, "Motherfucker, don't you ever think you can tell me to be quiet. Who the fuck do you think you are? Turn the fuck around right now." I was used to seeing my father act like that. Hey, it was his world.

About eleven years later, when I was attending the University of Southern California film school, a film called *Colors* had just been released. It was about two White cops in a Black neighborhood dealing with the gangs in Los Angeles. It wasn't a good movie at all. At a seminar where the film was being discussed, the patronizing producer said, "I didn't know that there were so many problems with the gangs."

This was pre–*Boyz N the Hood.* Back then I was formulating my ideas of what kind of filmmaker I was going to be and what kinds of films I was going to create. I was sweating and steaming, because I had grown up in South Central Los Angeles with people who were living with the problems associated with gangs. Seeing a condescending vision coming from a White filmmaker about my neighborhood had me mumbling to myself out loud. There were five to six hundred White people in the room, and maybe three Black people, none of whom spoke to me at all. The Black folks were the kind who don't speak when they're around White folks. It was that kind of deal.

Talking to myself, I said, "I can't believe this bullshit." A guy sitting in front of me said, "Could you keep it down, keep quiet?" I kicked his chair, and I said, "Motherfucker, don't you ever tell me to keep quiet. Who the fuck do you think you are? Shut the fuck up, now!" I sat back in my chair, and realized I was my father.

My life still revolves around the theater. Now I have a clear vision of what is special about me and my culture. That's why I ended up doing *Boyz N the Hood.* I define a story only I can tell. ∎

D'Angelo

OUR PEOPLE HAVE shown amazing strength and resilience over the years. We have faced and conquered injustices and triumphed in every industry imaginable. We have cultivated our own identity, our own society, and our own customs, and we have seen our ideas and culture permeate every sector of this society.

As a musician, I feel the passion, hope, despair, struggles, and triumphs of our people through our musical messages. It's Miles's horn crying a story, Parliament's sexed-out funk, Curtis's thought-provoking lyrics, and Marvin's leaving a phonographic legacy. Artistically, we capture our lives in the form of song that connects time and space, evoking feelings of the past. It's like when you hear a song on the radio today that your parents played at a barbecue, and it suddenly makes you hungry for ribs.

Music has a way of keeping life in perspective, creating change, and monitoring the pulse of society. Our music is a spoken legacy, much like the African oral tradition, and it continues to flow through our community like the blood through our veins. Our influence continues to dominate American pop culture, not just in music, where it is empirically obvious, but in film, fashion, and all other facets of this multimedia-driven society.

Among ourselves, we have a comfort zone that's sometimes unexplainable, but entirely familiar. Our collective identity belongs uniquely to us, a language that we don't have to speak, yet you know that you belong just from the eyes. It's about front porches and "speaking," and saying "Yes, ma'am." It's fried chicken and collard greens, church on Sunday, the dozens, and everything in between.

As the future unfolds, African-Americans will continue to have our spirit of growth, perseverance, aspiration, and recognition of our past accomplishments. And as each generation succeeds the next, it carries with it a legacy that cannot be replaced, misplaced, or erased. ■

With the release of his 1995 widely popular solo debut, *Brown Sugar*, Michael D'Angelo Archer put his personal stamp on soul music with his blend of R & B, rock, funk, and gospel. His second album, *Voodoo*, which he called his spiritual and mental musical journey, also went platinum. A consummate musician, D'Angelo plays drums, keyboards, guitar, and bass. He has recorded sound tracks and has worked with such talented musicians as Lauryn Hill and B. B. King.

T. S. Monk

After working with his father's jazz trio, drummer–bandleader T. S. Monk, son of legendary jazz great Thelonious Monk, ventured off in 1972 to form his own R & B group. In the early 1980s, after a series of personal challenges, including the death of his father, Monk dropped out of the music scene, devoting his time to the Thelonious Monk Institute, before he reemerged in 1991 with the T. S. Monk Sextet. Shortly after, he was struck with a bout of Bell's palsy, but he came back strong with 1997's heralded *Monk on Monk*, which won the 1998 Jazz Awards Recording of the Year.

WHEN I WAS a child, I didn't know what my father did for a living. I knew there was this music thing going on, and there were odd characters around, so I deduced that my father was in some sort of a cult. That was my first take on the jazz scene—strange guys, with Dad seemingly the strangest of them all. They lived and traveled in their own little universe.

I knew that my father played the piano, that he was famous, and that he was called "the high priest of bebop," but I still didn't get it. I remember Miles Davis would come to the door and ask, "Is Monk in? May I come in?" because he wanted to hear some tune. Ever since I was young, everybody said to me: "Do you know who your father is?" But to me jazz was his job—your dad might drive a bus, my dad played jazz. As a youngster, I would read music reviews from critics, and it affected me. One critic said, "He can't play," while another said, "He can't write." I realized that he seemed to play the piano completely differently from everybody else. The ugliness

inside me said, "Why doesn't Dad play like everybody else, so he can make the big cash and get on with his life?" But he kept playing the music he wanted to play.

I didn't realize my father's appreciation of music was rubbing off on me until I was fifteen years old. One day I came home from school and said, "Daddy, I want to play the drums." There was a forty-five-second conversation on the subject, highlighted by his saying, "You're late. You've got to learn how to read music and you need a teacher." That was it. He got me a set of drums, and then he called Max Roach. I overheard the conversation with Max, and it went something like, " Max, the kid wants to play drums and I'm sending him to your house." After that day, there was no mention of music again. There was no "Did you practice?," "Didn't you practice?," "You sound good," "You don't sound good," "It's too loud," "It's too soft." Not a word.

Several years later, when I was nineteen, I

decided I was going to build a speaker, although I wasn't knowledgeable about audio equipment. Afterward, when I needed to test the speaker, I didn't want to blow it out with my new Sly Stone or Temptations records. So I played a Monk Trio record. I turned it up and put my head down to the speaker to hear it, just as a great, tricky little composition called "Work" came on. I'd been playing drums for about four years at this point, so I was musically aware, but something caught my ear that made me say, "What was that?" I went back to the beginning of the record and listened again. I wondered, "How did Daddy just play that?" I spent the next two and a half hours replaying the tune again and again, marveling at his technical prowess and the genius of the melody.

Growing up around my father was perfect, because he let me dig on my own. He didn't get in the way. It's so simple that it's beautiful. He gave me room to grow and learn. How do you get a kid in? You do it by staying out. He used to say, "Man, you get stuff through osmosis." When I got to my first high-school biology class, I gained a deeper understanding of what osmosis is. It is absorbing what flows around you, so that you unconsciously know and understand it. I realize now that most everything I know about jazz—and about how and why we play this music—I got by osmosis. ∎

"Ever since I was young, everybody said to me: 'Do you know who your father is?'"
—T. S. Monk

Khephra Burns

in Compton, California, and went to an all-Black, all-boys school in Watts. Among my contemporaries, jazz was a rite of passage that came with puberty: It was men's music. Our counterparts at the local coed high schools didn't make that transition to jazz with us. They listened to Motown. And so did we when the sisters were around, but that was purely a concession to the dictates of teenage hormones. We knew enough not to insist on jazz in their company. That would have been tantamount to taking a vow of chastity. When the sisters showed up, radios quickly skipped down to the R & B end of the dial and Smokey Robinson singing "Ooo Baby Baby." But left to ourselves, we stayed tuned to Monk, Miles, and John Coltrane.

Trane was the last word among those who knew. In conversation, brothers would simply call his name and nod their heads knowingly as if, like adepts of a secret society, they shared knowledge that couldn't be communicated to the rest of us. Just as the preference for jazz separated the men from the boys, Coltrane's music separated the cognoscenti from the uninitiated. I was of the latter camp and skeptical. After all, if it was just music, how deep could it be?

The first time I heard Trane it seemed to me I'd walked smack into an impenetrable wall of noise: The tenor saxophones of Coltrane and Pharoah Sanders were screaming out of the box at Sam's Record Shop on Compton Boulevard. At fourteen, I was sure that whatever I was hearing wasn't music but the agonies of a tortured soul, and I loudly denounced Coltrane as a charlatan. It would be many years yet before I understood that it is possible to look and not see, to

Khephra Burns is a multitalented writer whose work spans books, magazines, television, and music. He has written the books *Black Stars in Orbit* and *Mansa Musa, Lion of Mali* and is coauthor, with his wife, Susan L. Taylor, of *Confirmation: The Spiritual Wisdom That Has Shaped Our Lives.* Burns is the author of several original works for stage and screen. He has written prime-time news specials on the plight of Black people for ABC and NBC, and is a cowriter and a coproducer of the televised Essence Awards.

listen and not hear, years before I understood how the judgments we make in our ignorance can return to indict us later, making us cringe in embarrassment.

I was nearly twenty-one the next time I heard that recording—a suite entitled "Love, Consequences, Serenity"—and had all but forgotten the fourteen-year-old know-it-all, the outspoken critic of my adolescence. I had since discovered other music by Coltrane—"My Favorite Things," "Olé," "A Love Supreme"— but this was different. And this time I *heard* it. Sitting alone in a second-story window, I heard Trane as I'd never heard anyone—not as a musician playing an instrument, but as a man who was himself an instrument of God. From the first

notes, he conveyed the kind of unconditional love, compassion, and tenderness a mother might express for her newborn baby in a gently rocking lullaby; a love that religions and mystics can only talk about; a universal, transcendent love that embraced all of humanity. In the passage where I'd once heard chaos I now felt the pain of our separateness and longing for union with the God of love and with one another.

Here was a man standing naked before the world, baring his soul for love's sake, even to the barbs of his critics. The gift he offered was rare and precious and exceedingly beautiful. And it had been there all along. The music hadn't changed, I had. And, like Peter after the cock crowed for the second time, I wept. ∎

"Here was a man standing naked before the world, baring his soul for love's sake..."

—Khephra Burns

Avery Brooks

Actor, director, musician, and educator Avery Brooks has achieved numerous triumphs on the stage and television. He has performed in Broadway plays, and his television credits include distinctive roles on *Spenser for Hire, A Man Called Hawk,* and *Star Trek: Deep Space Nine.* As a musician, he has performed with many notable jazz artists and sung the title role in the American Theatre Production of the opera *X: The Life and Times of Malcolm X,* as well as acting in several other productions. Brooks has taught at colleges and universities, including Oberlin College and Rutgers University.

MY BROTHER AND I were blessed with extraordinary parents. They grew up in Mississippi, deep in the Delta, then moved to Indiana, where they raised their family. My mother was a musician—a pianist, organist, choral conductor, and teacher, and my father had an extraordinary singing voice. Because of the strong influence of music that was all around me, expressing myself and performing came naturally to me.

Sometimes my mother would tell me, "You're going to speak in front of the congregation at church next week." That's the way she was. She never said, "Do you want to sing?" She just said, "Sing." I never hesitated about becoming an actor, because expression was always part of my life. I've come to recognize that expression is endemic to our culture. Among African peoples, there is music, there is movement, there is dance, there are oral traditions. It's the way we walk on the planet—a statement of our culture.

Working as an actor and a musician has led me to a myriad of places around the world. It has been incredible watching people's reactions to music. Some people have only just discovered that there is a healing quality to music. If you look at our musicians who have worked for any length of time and have survived the demands and obstacles of an artist's life in America, while also dealing with bigotry toward brown people, then you realize that this is an extraordinarily healing and powerful force.

The arts are merely a way to celebrate and preserve our culture, which is as critical as any other kind of sustenance that we require to stay alive. Like water. Like air. It's a force that nourishes and completes life. ■

Bill T. Jones

I BELIEVE IN art. For me art performs a function similar to that of religion. It helps me organize and mediate a seemingly chaotic universe. I make art—I am a performing artist, choreographer, and director. Though my parents were field workers, I chose to go into this expressive, metaphorical realm of living. This for me is not only a way of making a living, but a means by which I develop spiritual strength.

Through my work, which at its best is a discipline and a form of meditation, and by concentrating on the daily practice of living, I strive to strengthen my mind and understand spirit. We all must learn how to properly balance the conflicts

inside each of us in relation to the hypocrisies, the inconsistencies, and the mysteries of the external world. We must learn how to connect with the world on a social and ecological level even as we struggle with questions and doubt.

As a public speaker, I am often asked how one can live in this world of challenges and uncertainties. While not an authority myself, I have had the privilege of working with persons dealing with life-threatening illnesses who were generous enough to share their insights about how to develop the will to live in this world with dignity. From my conversations with these survivors I identified five important points: Set realistic goals and be willing and able to change them, cultivate a sense of community, recognize a higher sense of purpose in life, relish small things, and live in the moment. ■

Ernest Crichlow

Ernest Crichlow is an
award-winning painter
and illustrator. After
studying with respected
artists such as Augusta
Savage and Romare
Bearden at the Harlem
Arts Center in the 1930s,
he was hired by the
Works Progress
Administration as a
teacher and a muralist.
He cofounded a nonprofit
venue for Black artists,
New York's Cinque
Gallery, with Bearden and
Norman Lewis in 1969.

IN MY LIFE as an artist and teacher, one of my fondest memories is of an eight-year-old girl in my class. She would come in and paint for about a half hour, and she wouldn't talk or let anybody talk to her until she had finished her painting. It would be almost the same thing each time: She would paint beautiful color-field paintings— nothing you could distinguish. Everything was mushed together, but you couldn't help but be excited by the color.

One day she came in and worked for only half her usual time, then she sat down doing nothing. So I went over to her and asked, "Aren't you going to finish this painting?" She said, "Well, Mr. Crichlow, it's finished." All I could see was a black mass and a blue mass. Usually she'd have about twenty different colors arranged on the paper in a fresh, stimulating way. There was never anything specific, but the colors always gave you this feeling of warmth, gaiety, and laughter.

I pointed to the top part of the painting, which looked bluish, and the bottom part, which was black, and I said, "I don't know. I'm a painter like you, and usually when we paint something we know what we're painting." She said, "This is very difficult to explain to you." She started with the top of the picture and said, "You see, this is the sky." I said, "Well then, the lower part is the water." She agreed, "Yes, it's the water."

I asked, "Well, what about the waves in it?" She said, "No, there are no waves." I said, "Well, what is in it?" She answered, "You'll see later." So we talked a little bit longer and finally she

said, "You see, Mr. Crichlow, this is a ship sink-ing. And when a ship is sinking, I don't think there's any sky, ocean, trees, fish, sails, or waves in the water. I just can't explain it to you, but it just doesn't happen."

Here I am getting ready to finish my excursion down here—life itself—and I wonder what I'm looking at when I look at paintings. Now when I look at a color-field painting, an abstract painting, or a mystical painting, I see something like what that girl saw at eight years of age. These factors make an artist real. It gave me a great feeling to think that I am now a mature man, thinking and believing in the science of the spirit like the little girl who was painting from her source, her soul. Whatever you call it, she had something that I—and all the great artists—are trying to get. ■

Gordon Parks

IN 1942, I went to work for Roy Stryker, who was the head of the Farm Security Administration (FSA), an agency set up by President Franklin D. Roosevelt to explore the problems of impoverished farmers throughout America. I was fortunate to have been assigned to its group of photographers. Joining FSA was a coup for me, having just started in photography. The photo laboratory consisted of seven White photographers who were considered the glamour boys and girls. Now they were taking on a Black glamour boy. Stryker didn't want to hire me at first, but Roosevelt's people convinced him that I could take care of myself. I didn't know whether I could or not, but I found out rather quickly.

Coming from Minnesota, I was shocked at the prejudice and discrimination that I found in Washington, D.C. Stryker, who was our mentor, sensed my disbelief, so on my first day he sent me out to see the city. He told me to put my camera on the shelf and go to Julius Garfinkel's department store to buy myself a topcoat, then go across the street to the restaurant and get some food. Afterward, he said I should go across the street to a theater, look at the film, and tell him what I thought of it.

When I went to Julius Garfinkel's, nobody

waited on me properly. I left there and went across the street to eat, and the waiter said, "Don't you know Black people can't eat in this place? If you want something, you have to go around the back." When I went to the theater, I didn't even get to the front door. By this time I was in a terrible mood, so I hurried back to the FSA building. Stryker looked up at me smiling and said, "Well, how did it go?" He already knew how it had gone. He asked, "What are you going to do about it?" I didn't know. He said, "Why did you bring your camera here? You can't photograph a bigot and write bigot under the picture. Attack the bigotry and the discrimination in a way that everybody will understand. Attack it with your camera. Talk to some older Black people who have suffered this for a long time. See what they have to say." Then he left for the day.

An older Black cleaning lady named Ella Watson was the only person left in the building with me. I asked her about her life in the Deep South. She told me about terrible things that had happened to her family. I was really saddened by her story. After I listened to her for about fifteen minutes, I asked her if I could photograph her. She said yes. By that time, I was so

Gordon Parks is an award-winning photographer, writer, filmmaker, and composer. He was the first African-American photographer to work at *Life* and *Vogue* magazines and to work for the Office of War Information and the Farm Security Administration. With *The Learning Tree,* based on his book, he became the first African-American to write, direct, produce, and score a film for a major motion picture company. He has published sixteen books, including four autobiographies, and he is a composer of orchestral music, film scores, and a ballet. As director of the hugely popular 1971 movie *Shaft,* he brought Black films to the forefront. Parks is truly a Renaissance man.

angry, I looked around and saw the American flag hanging from the ceiling and said, "Stand right in front of that flag." I thought of the painting *American Gothic* by Grant Wood, with the farmer standing next to his wife, pitchfork in hand. I told her to put the mop in one hand and the broom in the other and to look right into the camera. She shook her head and smiled. I showed the picture to Stryker two months later. He looked at it, laughed, and said, "Well, you've got the right idea, but you're going to get us all fired."

Years later, when I was on a plane coming from Hollywood, I saw that picture on the front page of the *Washington Post*. I thought it had been destroyed. When the plane landed in New York, I flew to Washington and went to the Library of Congress. They were holding the film, so I had a copy of the photograph made, and it has been with me ever since. It's one of my most popular pictures.

The picture became important because it convinced me that I could use the camera as a weapon, not only against bigotry and discrimination, but against everything that I disliked about the universe and America. I could also use it to show the things I loved in America, the people I loved, the people I knew needed help, and the people I could speak for who couldn't speak for themselves. It became a divining rod. ▪

FAMILY

I'll give you a silver dollar
if you'll learn The Creation.
Why eyes. Big eyes. My mother
had me saying The Gettysburg Address
in a boyscout suit. Why didn't you say
something else, old man. I never learned
by heart, The Creation, and that is the key
to all life. I strain now through the mists
of other life, to recall that old man's
presence.
I know we are linked in destiny and cause.
I know he is my guardian and deepest
teacher.
I stand on his invisible shoulders.
I look for his enemies to tear their throats.
I wish that he had told me about J.A.

Rogers and
Psychopathia Sexualis. I wish he had
showed me
his Mason Book.
Perhaps it would have meant another path.
It wda saved some time, some energy, some
pain.
But love is the answer we keep saying, only
love.
And in my grandfather's pained eyes I
remember only
the keen glint of divine magnetism. My
grandfather
loved me.

—Amiri Baraka

Isaac Hayes

As an innovator in American popular music, singer, producer, and Academy Award–winning composer Isaac Hayes has a long list of artistic achievements. He was the first African-American to win an Oscar for Best Musical Score—for the *Shaft* sound track, which also won two Grammys. Early in his career, Hayes became Stax Records' most prolific composer–producer–musician, and he cowrote scores of hit songs, including many made famous by Sam and Dave. He has gained even more notice as an actor, as an author, as the voice of "Chef" on the hit animated show *South Park,* and as a disc jockey on KISS-FM in New York City.

MY GRANDMOTHER accompanied me to the 1972 Academy Award ceremonies, where I won an Oscar for the sound track for *Shaft*. At the time, she was eighty years old. I had the privilege of honoring her that night in front of millions of people around the world. I had prayed that God would keep her here long enough to witness my success. That night she said, "Lord have mercy, I never thought I'd live to see this day." I got choked up because I knew exactly what she meant.

I had my staff dress her exquisitely. She had diamonds and a mink, and she even went to Beverly Hills for a professional makeup job and a pedicure. Everybody expected that my date would be a real fine babe, so people were shocked when I stepped out of the limousine with my grandmother on my arm. She was not nervous at all, but I was scared to death. Oh, how I envied her, because my mouth was dry and I was a bun-dle of nerves. But we walked down the red carpet with all the stars. As the fans in the stands waved, she just waved back like a queen—she loved it. I guess at eighty years old, she couldn't have cared less about being nervous. When she saw the movie and television stars, she hilariously referred to them by their characters' names. She had a grand old time that evening.

My grandmother and I went back to Memphis to a huge welcome. About six thousand people were at the airport with bands and a wonderfully huge fanfare. Then we were invited to Chicago by the Reverend Jesse Jackson and Operation PUSH. My grandmother and I visited with our people in many various communities, the Cook County Jail, and a hospital. The wonderful times we shared are sweet memories that will be with me forever. She is no longer here, but my grandmother's dignity, joy, and grandeur will always remain in my heart. ■

Carl Hancock Rux

THE HARDEST CHOICE I've ever had to make was deciding exactly whom I would allow to be my family. My biological mother is mentally ill and institutionalized in New York, and I have no idea who my biological father is. I was initially cared for by my maternal grandmother in East Harlem, in an extremely difficult environment filled with alcohol and other substance-abuse problems. Nobody had any money. My grandmother died when I was four years old, and after a brief and shaky formative experience living with a great-uncle and his wife, I became a foster child.

The Rux family formally adopted me when I was fifteen. My adoptive mother was an incredible person, and we had a wonderful relationship, though not a perfect one. Even though I never called her Mother and she never called me son, she may as well have given birth to me. When I was eleven years old and living with the Ruxes as

a foster child, she took me to the Liberation Bookstore in Harlem and bought me a book of Langston Hughes's poems. She had read a poem I'd written and said, "You are a writer." That was her gift to me. She died not long ago, and my adoptive father died four years before she did.

I had two brothers who were raised separately. As young adults we reunited, and I was really happy. We lived in New York and I was beginning to have a sense of family. But about a year after our reunion, one of my brothers died of AIDS. After I lost him, I decided that the family I have is the family I make, not necessarily blood relatives, not legal guardians, not foster families. My younger brother and I talk now that he's an adult. At twenty-five he is struggling with his anger, with identity questions, and with the isolation he and I both feel. I see the same anger in him that I used to have.

Holidays used to be especially hard. Once a

Poet and performer Carl Hancock Rux combines elements of poetry, music, dance, and theater to create his own unique style. A product of Harlem, New York City's foster-care system, and Columbia University, the prolific writer and playwright has published *Pagan Operetta,* a collection of poetry and prose. In 1999 his debut album, *Rux Revue,* was released. His plays have been staged at the National Black Theater Festival and the Key West Theater Festival.

buddy of mine invited me to his house for Thanksgiving Day. He had lots of brothers and sisters, his mother and father were still together, and there were cousins, nieces, nephews, grandchildren, and people hugging one another; everyone had a history, everyone could connect. I was extremely uncomfortable. I had to leave because I realized I'd never had the experience of being surrounded by family, and I couldn't handle watching them.

Once I began the hard work of resolving my own issues with family, I saw that I did have a family, the people who actually cared for me, who took time out to spend part of their lives with me, the people who mattered. It was a hard choice to make, to say "This is my family." I have one family, but I also have another one—a family I made, a family I created by choice, and they provide a nurturing and wonderful structure for me. Some blood relatives can have very negative energy and might not be positive for my life. I don't owe them anything. I don't owe them my attention. I don't owe them my life. I just don't owe.

As an adult male, I've felt the responsibility to learn as much as I can about my familial existence. Then I have to decide whether to write it, sing it, keep it to myself, or do whatever I want to do with it. I wrote a book, *Pagan Operetta,* and some poems and short stories about my family. I was questioned and quietly attacked for my writings. Some family members were angry that I divulged some very personal and painful things, but I think it was the writer Jane Austen who said, "I reserve the right to invade my own privacy." That's what I told them: "Ultimately, it's my life." ∎

"She had read a poem I'd written and said, 'You are a writer.'"

—Carl Hancock Rux

Ian K. Smith

I CAN REMEMBER the sounds and the faces, even the kaleidoscope of drab colors, as if it were yesterday. But it wasn't. It was seventeen years ago on a gray autumn day in a small New England town that counted fewer than ten thousand people in its population. I was there with my twin brother, Dana, my cousin Robby, and my mother, Rena. It was a Saturday afternoon, and we had courageously ventured to this rural farm community to participate in a town fair where vendors had gathered to hawk their goods.

At the time, one of Ma's three jobs was selling brass. Her full-time employment was as a secretary at a small energy company in Danbury, Connecticut, and at night she traveled in our old Mercury Cougar hawking Tupperware bowls and accessories. Our outing today, however, concerned her brass, and it took all four of us to lug that heavy brown-twill suitcase. Unlike other vendors, we didn't fool ourselves by creating unrealistic expectations about what we'd earn in this no-frills town. We simply came armed with modest hopes of earning enough money to cover the gas-guzzling Cougar's fill-up for the week.

Top: Dana, Ian;
bottom: Robbie

The fair's organizers had instructed some of the vendors to set up their booths in a large building sitting atop a hill. The luckier vendors were assigned a high-profile location on the town's center green. I don't remember exactly who gave us the good news that we'd be on the green, but I do remember seeing the twinkle in Ma's eyes when we learned that our location would be right in the middle of everything. Always the strategist, she explained to us that this meant we'd have the maximum flow of traffic and potential buyers.

Dana, Robby, and I immediately went to work setting up the card table, then unwrapping and polishing the brass pieces that had become our meal tickets. We took special care with the bigger items, because they had larger price tags. If we were lucky to sell a couple of the elephants or donkeys, we were sure Ma would share a small cut of the profits with us.

The weather turned out to be perfect for an outdoor fair, and as the sun began to fade below.

Ian K. Smith, M.D., has informed countless viewers with his medical and health reports on the *Today* show, the *NBC Nightly News,* and *Today in New York.* He has also written weekly newspaper health columns and served as a contributing medical reporter for *Time* magazine. A graduate of Harvard University with a master's from Columbia University, Dr. Smith attended the University of Chicago Pritzker School of Medicine and Dartmouth Medical School, where he founded a mentoring program for the school's minority students.

the horizon, our calculations were showing that the day had turned out to be reasonably successful. The brass hadn't flown off the table, but there had been enough purchases to make the trip worthwhile. Once again, Dana and I sat and admired our mother, the absolute center of our lives. She had always been more than a mother; she was also a father, a progenitor of unrestricted love and affection, the proverbial breadwinner and pillar of strength.

As dusk fell, most of the vendors had already packed up and begun heading home, but true to form, Ma waited until the end, determined not to miss a sale. As we began to disassemble the stand, a White man who couldn't have been more than thirty sauntered up to the table and began eyeing one of the brass-headed canes. Dana, Robby, and I began nudging each other, because these canes were among the high-ticket items, and selling one at the very end of the day would be the proverbial icing on the cake. We stood quietly as Ma went to work, smiling first, then taking the soft-sell approach, not trying to rush his decision. The man walked up and down with the cane a few times, checking to see if it suited his size.

Just when it all looked like the sale would be made, everything fell apart. The man started

laughing in mockery, flicking the cane back on the table. He looked at the three of us standing there and seemed to laugh even louder, almost as if he knew his deciding not to make the purchase was like taking food out of our mouths. Then he spoke the words that did us all in, "Like I was really gonna buy that piece of shit."

I could feel the veins bulge under my skin as I clenched my fist in preparation for an attack against this grown man. As he walked off with his disdainful swagger, Dana, Robby, and I discussed all kinds of scenarios for our revenge, everything from calling him bad names to throwing sticks at him. But Ma sensed our hurt and anger, and in a way that was a testament to her character, she quickly defused the situation. "It's all right, boys," she calmed us. "Don't let him get to you. There will always be tomorrow." Those simple words and the events of that late afternoon have replayed in my mind thousands of times when life has delivered those unfair blows. To this day, when I look into my mother's eyes, I think that her strength, her boundless courage, and her ironclad willpower have not only stood down the ever-present perpetrators of racism and sexism, but have also kept her head high, majestically towering above all else that seems so small in her great presence. ■

Jesse Jackson, Jr.

ONE OF MY favorite pastimes is fishing. My late grandfather, Julius Brown, used to take me fishing every time I visited him in Hampton, Virginia. From ages fourteen to about twenty-one, it was just my grandfather and me, because no one else in my family liked to fish. I learned some of the great lessons of life on a little rickety boat with Grandpa Brown.

He was a very religious man and knew by heart the biblical scriptures that dealt with Jesus, Peter, and fishermen. My grandfather spent a lot of time out on the boat reflecting on the theology of fishing and what Jesus was actually doing while spending so much time with fishermen.

Sundays after we went to church was a great time to go fishing—same message, same lesson.

Sometimes I actually learned more on the boat than I did in church. Grandpa said that Jesus recognized that fishermen needed faith. As a matter of fact, on one occasion Jesus demonstrated his faith to the fishermen by walking on water. Another time, he told them while they were fishing on one side of the boat to cast their nets on the other side. Grandpa drew many lessons from these stories.

Grandpa told me that not all fish pursue the same bait—and you must set your hook right. You can't fish with large hooks when you're fishing for small fish or with small hooks when you're fishing for big fish.

The long and the short of the little lessons I learned from Grandpa, as he began to apply

U.S. Representative Jesse Jackson, Jr., was sworn in to Congress in 1995 at the age of thirty as the ninety-first African-American elected to Congress. He was formerly the national field director of the National Rainbow Coalition, where he initiated nonpartisan programs to register and educate millions of new voters. Congressman Jackson is the coauthor of two books written with his father, titled *Legal Lynching* and *It's About the Money.* He is the author of *A More Perfect Union.*

them to the Bible, was that when Jesus said that he wanted to make fishers of men out of fishermen, he understood that most fishermen had these basic tools and an understanding of how to catch a fish. He wanted them to take those tools and apply them to humanity. He knew that his disciples—his fishers of men—would encounter people who didn't want to hear a sermon that day. He knew they would meet people who were recalcitrant and hardened in their ways. He knew that people who were sick tended to hear ministry differently than people who had the wind at their backs, that people struggling against a head wind needed more help—a different aerodynamic—than those who were born into privilege. Jesus had an understanding of the full gamut of human experience.

Spending that kind of time on the boat with my grandfather helped me develop a better appreciation of just how daunting a task fishing is. There's fly-fishing, where you stand in the water and try to trick a fish into biting an artificial fly. You have to be very clever and creative in order to do that. Then there is deep-sea fishing. You can't do that from the safety of a pier.

The farther out you go, the greater the risk and the bigger the fish. Do we want to just hang around the shore and fish for minnows and little perch? Or do we want to catch the tuna and swordfish?

When my father ran for president in 1984, he said he wanted to go out where the big fish were. He didn't want to just fish around the shore. That's what Grandpa was talking about. If you want to change health care and education, you're not going to do that sitting on your living-room couch with a six-pack watching the football game. You have to go where the big fish swim.

That's why I introduced a constitutional amendment to provide every American with the right to a public education and comprehensive and universal health care of equally high quality. Most Americans believe they have a right to a gun, but there are no constitutional rights to an education or health care. Going for a constitutional amendment is going after the big fish. In addition to lessons I learned from Jesus and experiences my father shared, my grandfather showed me, from the practical perspective of an African-American man, how to be a fisher of men. ■

Ronald V. Dellums

BACK IN THE mid-seventies, my wife, Roscoe, came to me and indicated her interest in having a foreign-exchange student stay in our home. As parents, we wanted to expose our three children to a culturally enriching and educational human experience. We specifically asked for a young Black African woman so that our kids, who at the time were about eleven, twelve, and fourteen, would have a big sister. On a variety of levels this would be a fantastic opportunity. I reminded my wife, however, that I was spending long hours in congressional sessions and travel-ing back and forth from California to Washington, D.C. Therefore, for twenty-four hours every day, she and our kids would be work-ing with the exchange student. But I thought it was a lovely idea, and we did it.

The student arrived, and to everybody's shock and amazement, and through some bureaucratic fluke, we ended up with a White South African youngster—at the height of apartheid. As the seventeen-year-old girl got over the shock of expecting to see a White family and finding us, and we got over the shock of expecting to see a young Black woman and finding her, we became part of an incredible story.

This White child of apartheid found herself living in the home of the guy who introduced the first piece of legislation to bring sanctions against South Africa. I was way out front on that issue, so the irony was absolutely amazing. But by the time this girl's stay was over, we literally had to pry her away from our family. There were many tears. She had changed so much that when she got back home, she joined the student resistance movement and was jailed for challenging apartheid.

Several months later Roscoe said, "That was an extraordinary experience, but I still would

Serving nearly three decades in the U.S. Congress, Ronald V. Dellums distinguished himself as the respected chairman of several House committees, including the powerful Armed Services Committee. Lauded as one of the most compelling and articulate speakers to serve in the House of Representatives, Dellums also served as chairman of the Congressional Black Caucus. He is the author of *Lying Down with the Lions: A Public Life from the Streets of Oakland to the Halls of Power* and *Defense Sense: The Search for a Rational Military Policy*. After his distinguished congressional career, he became president of Healthcare International Management.

like the kids to know a young Black woman, to have an African big sister—for the culture, the education, the experience, and the enrichment." I told her it was fine, and, incredibly, the same thing happened again. This time, a fourteen-year-old White South African girl who thought she was being placed with a White family came to live with us. The van pulled up in front of our house, and when she found out we were a Black family, she wouldn't get out. I'm sure she had some bizarre views about what would happen to her when and if she walked into our home, and she absolutely panicked. With lots of prodding and persuasion the student did move in.

Once more a wonderful human story evolved. We grew to understand that she and the other kid were also victims of apartheid—in a different way from the kids of Soweto, but victims

nonetheless. The two situations also gave us an opportunity to live out the reality of our politics, to give each of these young people the experience of living in a Black family with one member who was an official in the "national parliament," a situation totally antithetical to what was happening in South Africa. Both young women formed friendships with our kids and clearly learned to see beyond stereotypical views of African-Americans.

Both stories are incredibly compelling, once you get past the shock, irony, and humor. We never viewed the girls as pro-apartheid White South Africans; we saw them simply as two kids away from home who were also victims. All of us remember this as a wonderful time of challenge and an enormous opportunity for learning. ■

"...but I still would like the kids to... have an African big sister..."

—Ronald V. Dellums

"...they should make wise use of the time they're given here on Earth."

Torry Jabar Holt

IN 1997, MY mother, at age forty-three, passed away from cancer. Her death was the greatest turning point in my life, and it caused me to change my outlook and my mind-set. It taught me that life is very fragile and way too short. I try not to take anything for granted anymore. I try to be positive, to live each day to the fullest, and to really enjoy each moment. Now, I'm doing my best to accomplish all of my goals and dreams.

Since my mom's death, I've been reaching out to youngsters to let them know that their lives are precious and that they should make wise use of the time they're given here on Earth. I look to my mom's life for inspiration because she did so much in her forty-three years.

I'm establishing the Ojetta B. Holt Shoffner Cancer Foundation in honor of my mother. It's important to me that the foundation achieve its goals of providing free cancer screenings to families in need and educating people about the disease. I dedicate our successes to her to ensure that her name rings on. ■

"I wake up... and count my blessings."

Kobe Bryant

I SPENT EIGHT years in Italy, where my father, Joe Bryant, played basketball for an Italian league. I started first grade there, and we moved to Philadelphia when I was fourteen. Living in Italy was beautiful, because we had a chance to experience a different culture and see another part of the world.

When I was thirteen years old, I played in an Italian summer basketball league. I wasn't very good. In fact, I went through the whole summer without scoring one point. When I came home after the league ended, my father noticed my disappointment and gave me a big hug. He said,

"Son, I don't care if you scored zero or sixty, you'll still be our son, and we'll love you no matter what." Those words put things in perspective for me. From then on, I wanted to work harder than ever to perfect my basketball game.

Now that I'm in the NBA, I try to cherish every moment—whether it's on or off the court. I wake up in the morning and count my blessings. And though it can be hard, I try to trust my gut feelings and follow my heart. When I think back to that summer in Italy, I remember how much my father's wise words helped me to grow not only as an athlete, but also as a person. ■

Following his incredible leap from high-school basketball to the NBA, Kobe Bryant has impressed both critics and peers as a guard with the Los Angeles Lakers. Bryant's brilliant playing at both ends of the court is credited by teammates and sportswriters as one of the key reasons for the Lakers' success.

Randall Robinson

As the guiding force of TransAfrica for more than two decades, Randall Robinson has put his personal stamp on American foreign policy, fighting for human rights and democracy by lobbying in Congress, staging protests, and writing editorials. His committed advocacy was instrumental in the dismantling of apartheid in South Africa and the return of President Jean-Bertrand Aristide to Haiti. His best-selling book, *The Debt*, presents a potent call for reparations to be paid to African-Americans for the devastation of slavery.

MY PARENTS WERE completely devoted to each other and are great models to emulate. My father was a tower of strength and courage. When I was a child, I thought he was fearless. He was extremely moral. He taught at my high school and coached me in high-school basketball. He really believed that it wasn't whether you won or lost, but how you played the game. He lived by this cliché, and it had an enormous impact on me.

There was never a time in my life when I didn't know who I was supposed to become. I'm not talking about a job, because my parents never imposed their particular notions of ambition on us. But it was very clear that they had some sense of the kind of people they wanted us to become. Recently, while talking to my eighty-seven-year-old mother, it became clearer to me how important parents can be in the development of their children.

A picture taken around 1870 hangs on a wall in my dining room. My maternal grandfather, whom I knew well and who died when he was ninety-three, is in this picture with his entire family, including my great-grandfather and suc-ceeding generations. One of the men in the picture, my great-grandfather's brother, had thirteen children; all of them finished college. They were teachers and lawyers and accountants around the turn of the century. In spite of the viciousness of racism in North Carolina and Virginia, this man and his wife put all thirteen of their children through college! Even those in the picture who did not go to college became successful in one way or another. The photograph shows the strength of the models provided by those great-great-grandparents. When you trace our family tree, you see the contemporary success of cousins who became every kind of professional and who are doing good work.

Success starts in one's head: It starts with confidence, setting a course, and maintaining high expectations. I was fortunate to have strong parents who gave me that foundation and had high expectations of as well as love for their children—my father, with his great courage and his moral example, and my mother, who was much the same and who descended from a long line of accomplished people we knew from pictures. ∎

Sinbad

Earning his big break in show business on the television variety show *Star Search,* comedian Sinbad has appeared on television sitcoms including *The New Redd Foxx Show, A Different World,* and his own series, *The Sinbad Show.* He has been the host of *Vibe, It's Showtime at the Apollo,* and *Sinbad's Summer Jam Weekend.* He has appeared in a number of films, including *Necessary Roughness* and *Houseguest.* Sinbad is author of *Sinbad's Guide to Life: Because I Know Everything.*

IN NOVEMBER 1967, when I was in the seventh grade, I was cut from my basketball team, and I ran home crying. When I got there, my father asked me what was the matter. I told him, and I waited for him to feel sorry for me. Instead, he left the house, got in his car, and drove away. I got angry because I wanted some pity, but my father had something else planned for me.

When he returned home, my father went into the backyard. After about an hour, he told me to come outside. After resisting his request to go out, I shuffled my way into the backyard where, lo and behold, my father stood sweaty and dirty from digging a hole for a basketball goal. He had bought somebody's old hoop. Dad threw a basketball to me and said, "If you work hard enough, you can do anything you want. Now, show me what you've got."

Through the years, my father not only taught me how to play basketball on that court, he also taught me about dignity, patience, and believing in myself. The lesson he taught me that evening I would later read in a book on positive thinking: "If you want to become great at something, you have to forget what you are today and think about what you want to become."

It took another couple of years of hard work for me to get myself some serious game, but that's another story! I will always thank Dad for believing in me. ■

H. Carl McCall

I WAS FORTUNATE

to learn early in life that we don't have to be defined by our circumstances. Growing up in Roxbury, Massachusetts, I was poor and Black, and my father had left home. My prospects may have seemed limited, but I was blessed. I had big dreams, and all around me I had evidence that dreams could become reality.

Every Sunday, my mother took me and my five sisters to St. Mark's Congregational Church, where we were surrounded by images of African-American achievement, leadership, and success. We worshiped with Black lawyers, doctors, teachers, and government officials. They were people of prominence, and just by sitting beside us in the pews, they told us we could be, too.

The men of the church had the most pro-found impact on me. They were smart, sharp, and in control—the preacher, the ushers, and

H. Carl McCall has had a distinguished career, with more than two decades of public service. His offices have included New York State Comptroller, New York State Senator, Ambassador to the United Nations, President of the New York City Board of Education, and Commissioner of the New York State Division of Human Rights. Prior to his career in public service he was a vice president at Citicorp/ Citibank. In 1999, he was elected to the Board of the New York Stock Exchange.

even the chairman of the Sunday school, Ed Brooke—a young lawyer who later became the first African-American United States senator since Reconstruction. He and these men were a source of inspiration for a young boy who had no male role models at home.

Fortunately, the men of the church opened their arms and invited me to join their extended families. They nurtured and supported me by making sure I had the skills and resources to match my rapidly growing ambition. I owe much of my life's success to them.

It saddens me that the experience that defined my life could be lost with my generation. Congregations like St. Mark's are increasingly rare, as so many of us have left our communities. While I applaud the personal success stories and societal transformations that have made it possible for African-Americans to move to the best

neighborhoods in the country, I fear for those we have left behind. There are young people growing up today in Roxbury, Harlem, South Central L.A., and thousands of other communities who desperately need role models. They need to connect with people who can be examples and an inspiration to help turn their dreams into reality.

Those of us enjoying life's great riches have an obligation to remember where we came from and all the help we had along the way. It is our responsibility to give back so that those who follow us have the same opportunities we had. When I was growing up, I used to receive a welfare check. Today, I sign all of the checks issued by the state of New York. The men of Roxbury made this transformation possible. They showed me a world beyond my circumstances, and they helped me to get there. My debt to them can only be paid in kind. ■

Walter Mosley

Walter Mosley is a critically acclaimed author of mysteries, short stories, science fiction, and screenplays. Mosley's novels have been on best-seller lists, and several have been made into motion pictures, most notably *Devil in a Blue Dress* from his Easy Rawlins mystery series. He wrote the screenplay for the HBO television movie based on his story *Always Outnumbered, Always Outgunned.* He helped increase the presence of minorities in publishing by founding PEN American Center's Open Book Committee, as well as by creating a publishing certificate program with the City University of New York. Mosley serves on the board of several organizations, including TransAfrica and the National Book Foundation.

BY FAR, THE greatest influence in my life was my father. He was a very complex person with deep psychological problems that stemmed from his childhood. His mother died when he was seven, and soon after, his father disappeared. By the time he was eight, he was already on his own, taking care of himself in 1920s Louisiana.

Hearing his story would make some assume that his early experiences should, or would, have caused him to be a very mature man. But he never really got beyond being eight. That's the age when you start to define yourself. That's when your dreams begin—everything starts at eight years old. But his real childhood and his dreams for the future ended there.

My father didn't know how to raise a child, because he never experienced the bond of the family unit beyond his early childhood. But he loved me passionately. In spite of all his problems he *loved* me. His love was unconditional. No matter what he did, no matter what I did, I was sure he loved me. Because of that, my father was a great man in my eyes.

Along with being a fountain of strength, he was an extremely bright man. I learned a lot from him about what to do and where I could go with my life. Life lessons that he never understood himself, he actually taught me—which is a wonderful thing about learning: You can teach something that you don't know yourself.

For the rest of my life I'll seek out fragments of my father in other people. His presence will always be with me. The gift of his unconditional love is a legacy I strive to emulate in my own life. ∎

Eddie George

Regarded as one of the elite and dominant running backs in the NFL, Eddie George made league history when he became only the second back in history to rush for more than 1,200 yards in each of his first five seasons. Tying the mark of being selected for the Pro Bowl four consecutive times, the 1995 Heisman Trophy winner earned Rookie of the Year honors from the Professional Football Writers of America (PFWA), *The Sporting News,* and *Sports Illustrated* in his first year with the Oilers, who during the 1999 season moved to Nashville and became the Tennessee Titans.

SINCE MY SON, Jaire, came into my life, I have grown spiritually and I'm finally learning what it takes to become a man. My situation is similar to that of most young Black fathers. I didn't plan to become a father this early in my life, but I'm glad it happened. It was definitely in God's plans for me. I've accepted that and I've taken on the responsibility to help nurture and guide Jaire through life. I am nurturing my son physically, mentally, and spiritually, not only because it is my duty, but also because I enjoy having him in my world.

Not being married to Jaire's mother has posed a challenge and at times the situation has been very difficult for both of us. The biggest issue is how each of us can spend as much time as possible with Jaire and juggle our schedules to make that happen. But we know what's required: communication and understanding. The ultimate issue is the welfare of our son, so we have to put our egos and motives aside to work together for Jaire. We have had to take ourselves out of the equation and look to what is best for him. I will support him in every way and guide him through his life's journey.

Since Jaire's birth in 1997, life for me has been a constant learning experience. As he grows, I grow too. Being a parent has given me a better understanding of the give-and-take of the parent-child relationship, and has made me a better son—a more understanding one—to my own mom and dad. My relationship with my parents didn't stop once I left their home. Even now, it's constantly growing and changing. It's a continuous evolution from infancy to adolescence, from adulthood into maturity.

As a father and son, I've come to realize that what's most important in life is the love you give and receive. I value life and the people in it so much more. Life is about loving, caring, and helping each other reach our maximum potential. My parents do that with me, and I intend to do it with Jaire. ■

FRIENDSHIP

Who are you?
A lost brother.
A singer. A song
I lost, almost, sat up
one night, itched
till it came
to me, cried
one night, happy
that it played
through me.
Little Brown Jug. Nigger Brother.
Dust singer in
the shadow of old
fences. Companion, of melody
rhythm
turned around heart runs
climbed & jumped screaming

WE ARE GODS, as we
sailed years through the firmament
landing beside a
garage, Dear brother, song
slides the streets, circles the cold,
sweats on summer fruit, Oh I
love my black energy &
lost brother father serenade
me, as world-solo, the spirits
bubble loft, & say
where you are. I suffer
to hear you so tough
& know all the spooks
who need to.

—Amiri Baraka

Bobby Rush

DURING THE CIVIL Rights Movement, my closest relationship was with Fred Hampton, who was murdered by police on December 4, 1969. I was always moved by his power, his charisma, his humor, and his courage.

One hot, humid Saturday evening at our un-air-conditioned headquarters at 2350 West Madison in Chicago, we had the windows raised to get whatever cool wind was circulating. I was sitting on the windowsill looking down at the hustle and bustle of the street when all of a sudden an argument started between Fred and several individuals who were standing downstairs. The disagreement wasn't entirely surprising, as we had a reputation for cleaning up our block, making sure that there were no drug dealers and no disrespect to the elderly or women. We didn't allow any of that nonsense to occur within the boundaries, or the surrounding area, of our office—the Black Panther Party headquarters.

Some gang-bangers joined the others and surrounded Fred. The argument got pretty heated, and there was posturing going on. Fred positioned himself to fight all four of them. They didn't see me upstairs, but I saw what was developing so I jacked a round into the chamber of a shotgun. They heard it and looked up.

When they saw me, they immediately cooled off and left. Fred came up the stairs, we embraced, and he said, "You've always got my back."

Love between two males is a special kind of love, because it's often raw and powerful. It's a motivating kind of love. It manifests itself through putting your life on the line for each other. It manifests itself through laughter—whether you're playing the dozens or sharing common experiences or joking about someone else. But it's also a commitment to throw down for each other. If you know somebody has got your back like that, to you he's a very special person. Fred and I had a special relationship because he would throw down for me, and I would do the same for him. Although he has been gone for more than three decades, his dynamic presence remains in my heart. ■

Congressman Bobby L. Rush is in a powerful position as a member of the U.S. House of Representatives Committee on Commerce and three congressional subcommittees, a position that allows him to participate in nearly three quarters of all bills considered in Congress. He has been the chairman of the Congressional Urban Caucus and a U.S. delegate to the North Atlantic Assembly, a parliamentary arm of NATO. A former member of the Student Nonviolent Coordinating Committee (SNCC) and cofounder of the Illinois Black Panther Party, Rush has dedicated his career to securing civil and human rights for all Americans.

Opposite page (left to right): Bobby Rush, Fred Hampton

Nas

WHEN I WAS about eleven years old, my friend's mom overdosed on drugs. The same day, the Bureau of Child Welfare came to take my friend away because he didn't have any relatives to take care of him. When my other friends and I realized that the BCW would be coming soon to move him, we went to the store and bought potato chips, popcorn, and other stuff, then stood together in front of his building in Queensbridge, Long Island City, New York, until he had to leave. When it sank into our heads that this might be a permanent separation, our little team of five guys realized how much we cared about one another. Tears poured down our faces because we thought we'd never see him again.

We missed him over the years but always held him in our hearts. Our crew often imagined how tight we would have been if he had stayed. We hoped to see him again and wondered where he was and how he was doing.

I saw my friend again about seven or eight years later in Washington, D.C. He had migrated there and was living his life. I was at Howard University for the homecoming parade, football game, and parties when I bumped into him. He wasn't going to Howard; he was just there having fun, too. We reminisced for a while, talking about old memories.

Caught up in the excitement of seeing each other, we shared stories of what we had missed over the years. Then I realized there was nothing else to talk about, because we were two grown men living two different lives. I decided that it was time to go. That was the last time I saw him. The encounter showed me that nothing is forever and that life is an unpredictable learning experience. Sometimes people come into your life for a brief period of time. You care about them, but circumstances change and your lives change. I learned that day when my childhood friend and I met again that you can't go back in time, that life gives you people and things and takes them away, too. You just have to keep moving forward. ■

Nas, the rapper, poet, and lyricist, is credited as one of the leading innovators among hip-hop artists. Born Nasir Jones, his breakthrough albums include *Illmatic* and *It Was Written.* His vision continually expands further into the reaches of hip-hop, from ghostwriting for Grammy Award–winning Will Smith to cowriting and starring in the film *Belly.*

As an international entertainment and multimedia lawyer, E. David Ellington developed NetNoir, Inc., an on-line company that creates and distributes Black programming and commercial applications for interactive media. Ellington's international expertise stems from his travels throughout Africa, Asia, the Caribbean, and Europe.

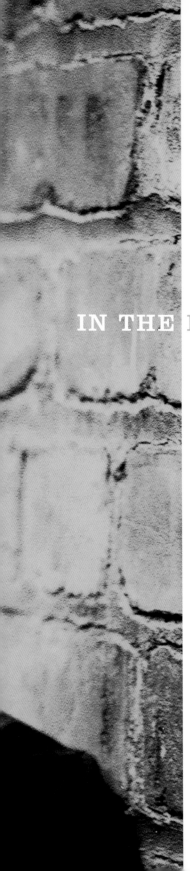

E. David Ellington

IN THE MID-EIGHTIES I back-packed around the world. Whenever I could, I'd try to hook up with other brothers in different countries, but there weren't many of them around. Unfortunately, few Black Americans really travel and explore the world. Some of my best experiences have come from bumping into the ones who do. Not only did we have fun, but we also developed really strong relationships, some of which I maintain to this day.

In 1987, while traveling in Asia, I met a brother in Hong Kong. I said, "I'm going to Thailand; why don't you come hang out with me on the beach down there?" He agreed. I went to a small island in southern Thailand, and he showed up a couple of weeks later.

He was a physically fit, tall, dark-skinned brother with locks. He used to play basketball and, like me, he had attended Howard University. At the time, I still drank alcohol and ate meat, but he was a vegetarian. One day we were out on the beach, and we met two very attractive young women who had been sitting on the shore watching us bodysurf. It was an absolutely beautiful eighty-five-degree day. There wasn't a cloud in the sky. The water was a brilliant crystal-blue that complemented the sky's radiance. As we watched and absorbed it all, it was almost as if we were high—but we were on a natural high.

At one point he stood up and said, "David, look at this." I said, "Yeah, this is amazing." He said, "No more intoxicants, David." At that moment I knew he was right: I didn't need anything else for stimulation. Right then and there I decided to become a vegetarian, and I stopped drinking alcohol. Who would have guessed that halfway around the world I'd meet a brother who would have one of the largest influences on my lifestyle? ■

Samuel L. Jackson

BACK IN 1982 when we first started to rehearse *A Soldier's Play,* which eventually became the film *A Soldier's Story,* there was a special feeling that we were doing something really interesting and exciting. A wonderful group of men were brought together to perform this play, and by the time the play was ready to open, an amazing bonding had occurred. The brothers and the White guys acting in the play became a family unified in a very special kind of way. Through doing that play, I developed lasting relationships with people who are still very close to me and still part of my family.

Eugene Lee, who was in the original cast, is now part of my everyday social circle in Los Angeles. When we all lived in New York, Eugene, his wife, and his daughter spent Christmas, Thanksgiving, and every other holiday at our house. James Pickens, who was also in the play, is a very integral part of my intimate family. We play golf together often. Brent Jennings and his kids share a lot of time with my family. We're also still in touch with Steve Jones, and with Denzel Washington, who has gone on to do all kinds of wonderful things. All of these brothers continue to work, and they are very viable because of *A Soldier's Play.* We all gained a sense of confidence about who we were, what we were capable of doing, and the power of what we could create.

It was a great group of men working together and gaining confidence through our director Douglas Turner Ward, a very nurturing and caring individual who made us feel that we were doing something special, and Charles Fuller, who wrote the wonderful play for us to perform.

Actors Adolf Caesar and Larry Riley, both of whom have passed on, and Peter Freedman and Carter Smith, two of the White guys in the play, did great things in their careers. All these guys and the rest of the cast became one solid unit when we were together back in the 1980s.

We did the show in New York for a year and a half, then several of us went on tour for eight months to two years. Through that experience, the strength of our relationships grew to the point that we felt like brothers. Today there is a "closed society" of men who were part of *A Soldier's Play,* and it makes us feel very special—because of the things we've accomplished, and also because of that lasting bond. ∎

As one of Hollywood's most sought-after actors, Samuel L. Jackson made a mark on American cinema with his memorable performances, including *Jungle Fever,* for which he won Best Supporting Actor awards from the Cannes Film Festival and the New York Film Critics. His vast list of film credits shows his phenomenal popularity with both filmmakers and audiences. Earlier in his career he performed in numerous stage plays, including *Home* and *A Soldier's Play.*

Cuttino Mobley

ALVIN WILLIAMS, JR., who also plays basketball, has been my best friend since childhood. When we were growing up in Philadelphia, Alvin and I did everything together. If one of us went out alone, folks would laugh and say, "Where's the other one?" As teenagers, when other kids were partying on Friday and Saturday nights, Alvin and I were in the gym playing basketball.

Alvin has helped me make some of the most important decisions in my life. During my teen years I didn't know what I was going to do with my future. I knew I wanted to play ball, but I wasn't focused. Once Alvin took me aside and said, "Man, you have to get yourself a goal and a dream."

At first I didn't listen, but then I sat back and thought, *You're right. I do.* He said I was either going to accomplish my goal or I would stay at home with everybody else. Those words really hit me. I thought: *I can always come home. I can always hang out with my boys. But I'd do a lot better if I had my degree, money in my pocket, and* success. That's when I discovered my dream was for both Alvin and me to graduate from college and play in the NBA.

I remember the night Alvin was drafted—a year before I was. That night, the first round of the NBA draft went by and Alvin's name wasn't called. Then came the second round, when choices thirty to fifty-eight were announced. Alvin and I became even more nervous. Alvin's name was finally called as the forty-seventh pick. We jumped around, hugged, cried, and I said to myself, *Next year it's my turn.*

Our goal was crucial to us, because that's what we had been striving for, but to other people this whole situation wasn't that important. The next year we were in the same predicament—this time sitting in my house, heads down and waiting. When they called my name, everything happened again; it was like déjà vu. These were the times when I learned how important it is to have friends, and that you stick with them—no matter what. God gives you only a few real ones. ■

Cuttino Mobley seized the attention of NBA recruiters in 1998 as the NCAA Atlantic Ten Player of the Year for his outstanding performance at Rhode Island University. He went on to join the Houston Rockets as a guard and continues to delight basketball fans with his aptitude for high score averages and above-average free-throw percentages.

Ron Carter

SO MANY PEOPLE

Grammy Award–winning Ron Carter is among the most original and influential bassists in jazz. With more than three thousand albums to his credit, he has recorded and toured with music's greats, including Lena Horne and Cannonball Adderley, and was a member of the legendary Miles Davis Quintet. He has scored, composed, and arranged music for films. Carter also authored a series of books, including *Building a Jazz Bass Line*. He earned a master's degree in double bass from the Manhattan School of Music in New York, by which he was awarded a Ph.D., and has served as a distinguished professor of music at the City College of New York.

I knew in my age group are no longer among the living, and the older I get, the more passionate I become about renewing past relationships that have been lost. Most accomplished musicians have had great experiences with men of distinction, but the competitiveness of the industry demands that you look out for yourself. It isn't that you aren't concerned about other people, but your first priorities are making gigs, playing as well as you can, and developing a reputation as a professional. You must be prompt, play great music, dress correctly, and take care of whatever business is necessary to make the job a musical and financial success.

In trying to cover all these bases adequately and for our own protection, musicians may sometimes act in ways that don't inspire trust or bonding between us. We may not always say good night to one another, or we may not always consider whether the choices we are making in a situation are tenable to both parties. These are some of the things that can strain our relationships.

Musicians in my age range are leaving this Earth more quickly than ever, so I've made it a point over the past several years to call the people I care about and have enjoyed working with to say hello.

Every Christmas I call Herbie Hancock and Wayne Shorter to wish them and their families well. That simple act helps to continue our relationships. During the holidays, I sit down with my telephone book, starting with the letter *A,* and call people whom I haven't seen in a while, or whom I know I won't get around to sending a card to. I've made a conscious effort in the past several years to bring back on the horizon those relationships that have faded.

It doesn't always work out. Not everyone is amenable to rekindling relationships. Some people don't return your calls. They think you've got a game going or that you're not really serious.

In the jazz world, everyone may respect everyone, but they're reluctant to share feelings, to say "I missed you last week; I did a concert and I thought about you." We're all guilty of sometimes not expressing those kinds of thoughts, and I regret not doing that with some people.

Recently, I saw drummer Grady Tate for the first time since last summer. We've made many records and played lots of gigs together. He said, "Hey, man, I love you and I miss playing with you." It gave me a great feeling to know that he is comfortable enough to say that. I'm getting more comfortable, too, and more passionate about expressing my love as the years go by. ■

Ron Carter in Harlem, 1998.

Tony Dungy

I WAS TWENTY-ONE when I left the University of Minnesota and joined the Pittsburgh Steelers in the late seventies. As a rookie I was trying to find my identity, so I was susceptible to all of the pitfalls that accompany life as a pro athlete. But I was fortunate that some of my teammates—Joe Greene, Dwight White, J. T. Thomas, Donnie Shell, and John Stallworth—took me under their wing. They were prominent players who had won several Super Bowls and whom I had watched on television. But they still took time to teach me about football, my role as a Black man, and the importance of having a balanced life.

Being around these supportive men gave me a sense of what was required of me. I used to ask John Stallworth about the proper way to dress. He told me what to look for in clothes and how to carry myself. John even took me shopping—a gesture I've never forgotten. Sometimes these guys teased me because I was pretty naïve, but they never allowed me to continue behavior that was harmful to me. They showed me the proper way to deal with the media and fans and taught me to be more forceful and outgoing. They gave me advice that helped build my confidence— and that serves me well to this day.

These men also made a significant impact on me politically and intellectually. When I visited Joe Greene's room, I'd find him, Mel Blount, and Franco Harris discussing issues like affirmative action and politics—things I hadn't even

Considered one of the National Football League's top defensive minds, Tony Dungy transformed the Tampa Bay Buccaneers into a young powerhouse team as head coach. In addition to his success with the Pittsburgh Steelers and Minnesota Vikings, he has been active in community service with the Fellowship of Christian Athletes and Mentors for Life organizations. From Tampa Bay, he went on to coach the Indianapolis Colts.

thought about. They were very involved in the community and in starting businesses and were looking toward finishing their football careers and getting into other areas. I was so focused on football I couldn't even fathom the thought of life beyond the NFL. Through our conversations, these players encouraged me to broaden my horizons. They would ask: "What can you do to help the Black community and society?" or "Do you think you are just here to play and that's the end of it?" I had never thought about those kinds of questions.

It was Donnie Shell, though, who helped me put my life in perspective. In 1978, my second year, I had mononucleosis and couldn't play. I had gone about five weeks or so without good progress reports from the doctor. I talked with Donnie because I was very frustrated. He told me that I was putting so much emphasis on football that my spiritual life and my frame of reference for life were all screwed up. He said that until I was ready to put football in second place behind God, I'd always be frustrated. That was when I realized that football couldn't be the most important thing in my life.

Without the direction of John, Joe, Donnie, and the others, I would have been lost. These men were superstars, but even more important, they were gentlemen—Black men I truly admired. They helped me become the man I am today. ■

" …my spiritual life and my frame of reference for life were all screwed up."

—Tony Dungy

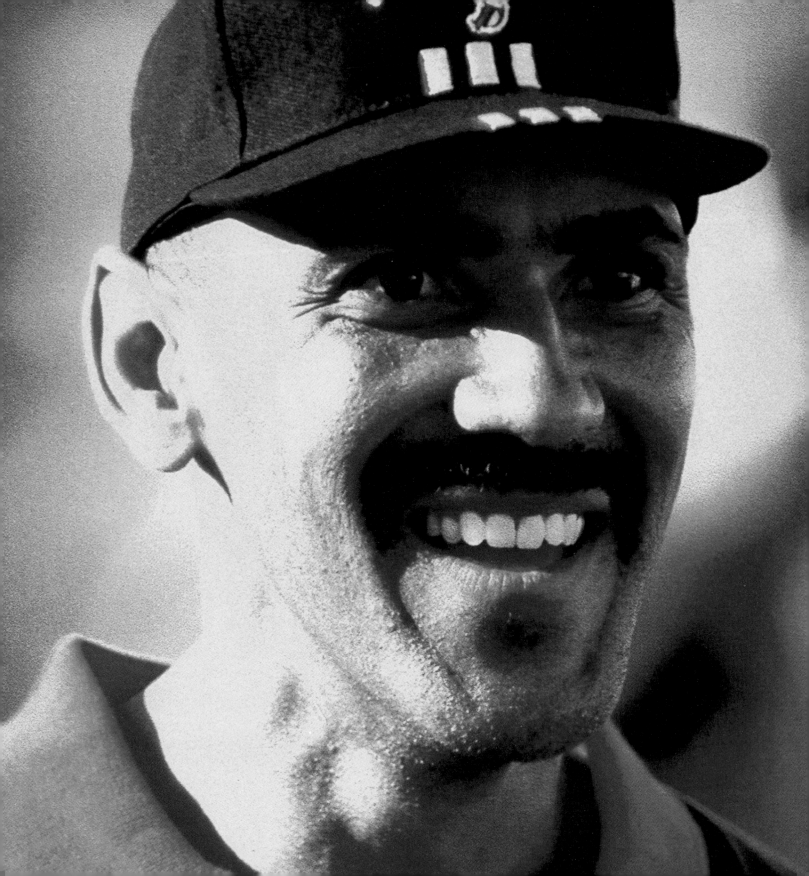

Earl Graves

AFTER THE SHOOTING of Amadou Diallo, a young unarmed Black man who was fired at forty-one times by the New York City police without cause, Ed Lewis, *Essence*'s CEO and chairman, and I agreed to go down to police headquarters to get arrested in protest. When we got there, we ran into Hughlyn Fierce, a prominent international banker and our good friend and fellow Omega fraternity brother, who had attended Morgan State University with me. Getting arrested is a serious thing, especially when you do it voluntarily. We were the first corporate executives to be arrested as a result of that tragedy.

We had been at police headquarters for about twenty minutes when another boyhood friend and fraternity brother, Professor Sam Pinn, came in. We told the arresting officer, "That's one of our friends; he's supposed to be with us." So the officer put the four of us in a holding cell together. We spent the morning and afternoon together reminiscing about the progress that we as Black people had made or not made in light of the Diallo tragedy. It was a time of bonding.

They took us from police headquarters to a local precinct in a paddy wagon, handcuffed to the inside of the vehicle. We could have been released when we got to the precinct, but the captain had decided that he wasn't going to let us go that easily. The police left us standing around for nearly two hours just to irritate us.

After we were released, we went back to my office for lunch and talked about the future. We asked questions like "How can we create better lives, not only for ourselves, because we're already the graybeards, but also for future generations?" We asked, "What can we do to overcome the tragedy of the police brutality we're protesting?" There we were—people who had gone to school around the same time, people who were in the same fraternity, Black men, all of us close to sixty years old or older, and we were singular in purpose. We hadn't planned to join one another that day, but we came together searching for answers, justice, and ways to ensure that what happened to Amadou Diallo never happens again. ■

Earl G. Graves, publisher of *Black Enterprise* magazine and the author of the best-selling financial book *How to Succeed in Business Without Being White,* is a national authority on Black business development. This former U.S. Army Green Beret was chairman and CEO of the largest minority-controlled Pepsi-Cola franchise in the United States. Graves was honored in 1995 when Morgan State University, his alma mater, renamed its business school after him.

SUCCESS

Craziness is no
Act
Not to
Act
is crazinezz

—Amiri Baraka

Jamie Foxx

BECOMING A COMEDIAN has always been in my blood. I was in the first grade when I realized it, and by the fourth grade I was doing a full stand-up routine in class. I would retell funny jokes I heard and do impersonations. Jimmy Carter was president then, so I would impersonate him and Tom Jones.

Television made a big impression on me when I was a kid. *The Jeffersons* inspired me. Watching George Jefferson, a Black man who wasn't afraid to call a White man honky on national television, was revolutionary. Redd Foxx ran his little junkyard kingdom, but he still made you feel like he was the king of the world. When Sammy Davis, Jr., guest-starred on *All in the Family,* he handled Archie Bunker. These shows helped me shape my point of view as a young man coming up.

The first time I stood onstage with legitimate comedians was at the Comedy Act Theatre. My first performance was like going up against the firing squad, because with Black people, if you're not funny, they'll let you know right away that you need to find a different line of work. I was introduced by the late Robin Harris, who was probably the best comedian I've ever seen live. As he was introducing me, he totally dogged me out and said I wasn't funny. He had everybody laughing at me. He said I wasn't on television, I had never had a television, and I had an extension cord running all the way to the liquor store. That crushed me, because I had been talking to him about how excited I was to be a comedian. I knew he was joking, but the way he roughed me up, I knew that I had to prove myself when I got onstage.

I went up and turned it around. I did an impersonation of him saying how angry he was, which was one of his classic routines. I got a standing ovation. Later he said to me, "If somebody can climb up from all I put on you, then you know you're on your way to being something." I began to understand that being a comedian is a rough business. I learned that it's like being an old gunslinger. It's like the OK Corral in the Old West—you better have your guns packed, ready, and filled with jokes if you want to succeed. ■

Multitalented Jamie Foxx has achieved success in stand-up comedy, television, film, and music. After gaining initial recognition on the television comedy *In Living Color,* where he showcased his signature mix of stand-up, impressions, and singing, Foxx starred in the *The Jamie Foxx Show.* Among his film successes is his groundbreaking dramatic performance in the feature film *Any Given Sunday.*

Vince Carter

WHEN I PLAY basketball, I always have a beat in my head. That's because music has been a big part of my life—from playing saxophone, trumpet, and a bit of drums to loving a wide range of music, including jazz and hip-hop—East Coast and West Coast. During crunch time, when the game is on the line, you'll see my head bobbing to a beat. The music makes me feel relaxed and calm.

At the 2000 All-Star Game, I tried not to put pressure on myself, although there was a lot of hype surrounding the slam-dunk contest. You could feel the excitement in the air. I was honored to have the opportunity to be with NBA stars and major slam-dunkers. But I approached the competition like I was out there with my teammates, fooling around, dunking in the schoolyard. I arrived at the arena early and sat around having a good time watching the other events that took place before the dunk contest. I was able to share that incredible experience with my cousin Tracy McGrady, who plays on my team and who was also in the contest. When it was my turn to go onto the basketball court, I locked in and focused on what I had to do to get the dunk.

I breathed a big sigh of relief when it was over, because by winning the contest I accomplished one of the major goals of my career. When we came off the court, Dr. J was the first person to congratulate me. Growing up, I had been a big fan of Dr. J when he was playing in the NBA. He added enormously to that wonderful day. It was truly a dream come true. ■

Russell Simmons

Russell Simmons created a hip-hop empire from his early vision of hip-hop as a future cultural phenomenon. In the early eighties he founded Rush Artist Management and helped mold the careers of artists such as Run DMC, Public Enemy, and Will Smith. He cofounded Def Jam Recordings in 1984, which developed into rap music's premier label. Seven years later he spawned HBO's *Def Comedy Jam,* which launched the careers of some of today's most dynamic comedians. He also started Phat Farm, a highly successful clothing line. As chairman and CEO of Rush Communications, he continues developing new ventures, including *One World* magazine, syndicated television, 360hiphop.com, and dRush advertising agency.

WHILE I APPRECIATE being characterized as one of the most successful Black businessmen, I also resent it. Most people expect less from us, so they'll pat us on the back rather than giving us the prize. I have a history of fighting to change the stereotypes surrounding Black Americans and Black American businessmen.

I don't care to make "Black movies" or be a "Black record executive," because I don't want a substandard budget and lower expectations. We've now proven that it's okay to say you're Black, although that statement may limit you later.

I'd rather not be considered the owner of a "Black advertising agency." I was for some time, despite the fact that my commercials are successful in the mainstream media. If 75 percent of the culture I sell is being bought by non-Black people, I don't want to be relegated to receiving a "Black advertising" budget. I don't want my business to be the most successful Black company; I want it to be the most successful *American* company.

There may not have been an opportunity before, but I believe that racism in this country has relaxed enough for us to start to exploit our own culture properly. We should not limit our marketing to our own community, because our ideas are pushing the whole mainstream and cultural press. When I talk about wanting to move my clothing line out of the urban-clothing section, it's not a desire to be someone else. I simply want to move on to being recognized as a designer. I want to create a billion-dollar company and compete on that level.

The mentality that limits us to marketing our products only to Black clients obscures the big picture. I have no desire to put pressure on people to give me an ad just because I own a Black magazine or to give me a section in their store just because I'm Black. Instead, I would rather encourage people to be open-minded about their choices and to give me what I deserve because I'm successful. I don't want to always scream things that will scare them. You can be a militant Black, proud and very sure of what you've been deprived of and what you want; you can be aggressive, because there's an important place for that. But your attitude doesn't have to be limited to: *Give us some shit. You owe it to us.* I don't want to use demands as my crutch or blame racism for not getting somewhere.

Some people automatically make assumptions and label me as some kind of "whitewashed nigger." I absolutely am not. I want all of the American pie that I see on television. It takes all kinds of people to make a movement. ■

Melvin Van Peebles

WHAT I'VE REALLY tried to do through filmmaking is to make it commercially feasible for us to have some say about the mirror that is us. In the past, other people told us who we were and defined our look, so that we saw only their perceptions of us. I'm passionate about making it possible for people to define themselves.

I never went to school for cinema, film, theater, acting, or music. I was self-taught. I realized that when I was working for fifty cents an hour I had to kiss butt. So why not do it for five hundred dollars an hour? What did I have to lose? I got a book on directing high school plays and read it so I'd know stage left and stage right. Then I knew how to tell people where to stand.

The first time I ever tried to do a movie was back in 1957 or 1958. It was called *Three Pick Up Men for Herrick,* and it was eleven minutes long. I thought it was a feature, but I didn't know about writing, and I'd never heard the word *editing.* I had no funding; I was working, so I just saved my lunch money, sold my car, and set out to make a film. I haven't had a car since.

When I decided to do *Sweetback* in 1971, no studio would touch it. I just asked myself, *What's a studio?* A studio is a name. One morning while shaving, I just said, "Melvin, you're a studio." When I started to figure out how much the film would cost, I calculated that I could do it for five hundred dollars. Of course now everybody's crying genius and saying, "Oh, you're such a financial wizard." I begged everybody in the world to help and invest in it. But nobody would, so I had to do it.

Then back in the 1970s when it came time to do the music for my play *Ain't Supposed to Die a Natural Death,* I felt the music I was hearing didn't embody urban reality. So I created my own, and that became what they now call rap. It was really the first rap. It was a series of monologues about our situation. I had to do the music because I couldn't afford to pay anybody to sing. I couldn't remember the melodies, so I just numbered all the keys on the piano. I still can't read or write music. I just play the numbers.

Doing it myself—that's how I made my mark. This has become the paradigm for many independent young filmmakers. If they look at me and my work and say, "He did it; maybe we can do it, too," that's very gratifying. I guess Nike says it best, although it was my philosophy thirty-five years earlier—*Just do it.* ∎

Freeman A. Hrabowski III

Freeman A. Hrabowski, III, president of the University of Maryland, Baltimore County, works tirelessly to recruit more minorities into math, science, engineering, and technology fields. He is a consultant to the National Science Foundation, the National Institutes of Health, and the National Academy of Sciences. He is also a member of numerous boards, including the American Council on Education and the Joint Center for Political and Economic Studies. Hrabowski is the coauthor of two books, *Beating the Odds* and *Overcoming the Odds*.

THIRTY YEARS AGO, I was preparing to graduate from Hampton Institute and begin my graduate studies in mathematics at the University of Illinois. What Hampton did for me was to build on the strong foundation my parents and community in Birmingham, Alabama, had given me throughout the 1950s and early 1960s. I recall my parents' saying that because I was special, much would be required of me. Although the larger society continued to communicate in so many ways that I was a second-class citizen, I was, in fact, a child of God with the ability to think critically and control my own destiny. My family, church, teachers, and neighbors all let me know that to be a Black male was a good thing and that I stood on the shoulders of giants. I will never forget how my father responded to me as a child when I hurt myself. He looked into my eyes, smiled, and said, "You can stand it if it doesn't kill you!" I thought he was being harsh, but I have come to understand that he was making me strong for the life ahead of me.

Growing up in segregated Birmingham, I felt a sense of urgency about needing to work harder than expected in order to achieve. I learned that I had to be twice as good as Whites because I could not assume the world would be fair. What was so positive about growing up where and when I did was that there was a loving, tightly knit community around me that applauded high academic achievement. Neighbors constantly heard about our grades, and when we did well, they told us, "Good job!" My pastor had those of us who made the honor roll stand while the congregation applauded enthusiastically. It was a good thing to be smart. One of the great challenges our community faces

today is to re-create a culture that rewards academic achievement and encourages our children to want to be smart.

As I reflect on my childhood, I see that one of the most important decisions my parents allowed me to make was to go to jail with Dr. Martin Luther King, Jr., as part of a civil rights protest in the early sixties. They helped me realize, even at age twelve, that I had to work to control my destiny, that I could not afford to consider myself a victim of racism, and that through my own actions, I could change the world. That experience was a turning point for me; it was then that my conscious journey into manhood began.

Thirty years later, I am more convinced than ever that my sense of self is tied to my willingness to work as hard as necessary to achieve any goals I establish—and it's tied to those giants on whose shoulders we all stand. ■

Byron Lewis

GROWING UP IN Queens, New York, when I did, I lived in a small enclave of Black folks who were recent arrivals from the segregated South. Our neighborhood was located on the other side of the railroad tracks that separated us from the wealthy and well-educated White community in my town. My father, mother, relatives, and neighbors all worked in service capacities for these people. I went to school with their children.

One day, my third-grade teacher asked my mother to come to school. I thought I'd done something wrong and I was scared to death. Times were tough during the 1930s Depression. In those days it was like death for a Black kid if your parents had to miss work to meet with your teacher, so you could expect the whipping of your life.

My mother was an intelligent, ambitious, and hardworking person. She understood the need for education but was extremely sensitive to seemingly patronizing attitudes toward her children. So when the teacher said, "Your son has academic abilities, but he's not living up to his potential, and you'll have to help open the world to him so he can do better," my mother felt the comments were insulting and was deeply offended. Nonetheless, she followed the teacher's advice.

For the next six months, my teacher had me do extra duty in all my subjects. My mother worked with me on my assignments. At first I felt really hampered doing so much work, especially when I saw the other kids in the neighborhood outside playing. But I didn't have a choice.

Byron Lewis, founder and CEO of UniWorld Group, is heralded as the dean of African-American marketing and communications. He has built UniWorld into one of the nation's largest ethnic advertising agencies, with an impressive roster of Fortune 500 clients. In 1996, Lewis founded the Acapulco Black Film Festival, which annually attracts numerous aspiring filmmakers, and he has been the executive producer for *America's Black Forum*, a national news television program.

My parents were the authority in our home so I hunkered down and did as I was told. In a short time amazing things began to happen: I began to enjoy school. My math and reading scores improved, and as a result of my intensive effort, I caught up with my class and skipped a grade. I also discovered that I could write and draw. As a matter of fact, I could do these things better than any of my wealthy classmates.

When my mother saw the difference in my performance she was so proud of me. In just a few months, my life had changed. Now I was a young Black boy feeling smart and confident.

There have been countless times as an African-American man trying to build an ad agency in a high-stakes business environment when I've drawn on the lessons I learned in the third grade. When we have to navigate the rough side of the mountain, we have to focus on the task at hand, dig our heels in, and keep putting one foot in front of the other. We have to summon the courage to keep doing the work. And when we do, the rewards—self-esteem and personal achievement—are always great. ■

"When we have to navigate the rough side of the mountain, we have to focus on the task at hand..."

—Byron Lewis

Dikembe Mutombo

I WAS BORN in the Democratic Republic of the Congo (formerly Zaire), and I came to the United States in 1987 on a USAID scholarship to attend Georgetown University as a premed major. It had been my childhood dream to become a medical doctor and return to my homeland to help my people. In my life I have had many challenges, but the biggest one I've ever had to face is the one I'm facing now.

There are now more than 10 million people in the capital city of Kinshasa, my hometown, and more than 40 million people throughout my country, which has some of the worst health conditions in Africa. Americans go to the hospital to get better, but my people, too often, go to the hospital to die. The Democratic Republic of the Congo is one of the last countries on the planet where polio and measles still threaten our children. Only 20 to 30 percent of young children are vaccinated against these debilitating, preventable diseases.

In 1997, I created the Dikembe Mutombo Foundation, Inc., with the mission to improve the health, education, and quality of life for my people. This is a big job, and I will need a lot of help. But all of my success in America would be pointless if I did not look back to where I came from and help the people there. When I move on through life and people ask me what I've done, what would I say—that I just played basketball?

To start the improvement project I donated $3 million. Our first endeavor is to build a 300-bed general hospital, then an elementary

school and a recreation center. We will establish partnerships with American universities and international organizations to help give our physicians and medical technicians the best and most modern training, which will prepare them to return to the Congo and offer the best medical support. The establishment of the hospital will ensure that people have a place to get medical treatment, deliver healthy babies, and be vaccinated against disease. The hospital staff will also teach people how to prevent many diseases that now seriously afflict them.

I am a fortunate son of the Democratic Republic of the Congo. I was educated at Georgetown University and I am a well-paid athlete, but I am only one of many gifted athletes in my country, most of whom are untapped on playgrounds and in villages throughout my nation. By building a recreation and sports facility, I hope we can develop the most talented Congolese athletes and attract scouts to recruit them. The center will also be a place from which we can offer community service and disseminate health messages to the public. All of this is my commitment. There's a Central African saying: "When you take the elevator up to reach the top, please don't forget to send the elevator back down so that someone else can take it up." This is my way of sending the elevator back down. ◼

Known for his work on and off the basketball court, NBA star center Dikembe Mutombo has donated time and money to improve educational and medical standards in his homeland through his Dikembe Mutombo Foundation. The Congolese native was awarded the United States' highest volunteer service honor, the President's Service Award, by President Bill Clinton.

Bill Bellamy

ONE OF MY most memorable moments occurred several years ago at the Comedy Store in Los Angeles. I was supposed to perform a fifteen-minute spot, and I was on edge because I was running a little late. When I finally arrived, I found out Arsenio Hall was hosting. That made me really nervous because he's one of my peers and a guy that I look up to. Immediately I thought, *Oh man, I've got to be really funny!*

As I walked toward the back of the club, I wasn't looking where I was going, so I bumped into a man. I glanced back and said, "Excuse me, sir," and I realized it was Richard Pryor. I thought, *You've got to be kidding me! I'm trippin' in more ways than one!* After I collected myself, I sat down in the corner to go over my notes before my set. When I looked up, I saw Eddie Murphy walking in. The pressure I was feeling really went over the top.

Everybody was there because Richard Pryor was performing that night, but I hadn't known before that moment that I would be performing in front of a star-studded audience. Everybody I had ever looked up to in the comedy game was in the room!

It was like being at an all-star game, where you have to play your best. So I just ripped it. I had an incredible night, one of the best sets of my life. Afterward I received compliments from Arsenio. And Richard Pryor, who went on after me, said, "That's a funny motherfucker!" Such an accolade from this comedy genius was incredible! He's the godfather. He's the Michael Jordan of comedy to me.

Seeing all these legends perform in the same room left me energized. And after I got the ultimate compliment from Richard Pryor, I was pumped with a boost of confidence like never before. ■

Comedian and actor Bill Bellamy's career has encompassed film, television, and comedy. After five years hosting *MTV Jams* with his unique combination of professionalism and charisma, the multitalented comedian began dividing his time between performing stand-up comedy across the country and acting in films such as *Love Jones* and *The Brothers*.

Bernard King

IT WAS NEAR the end of the 1984–85 NBA season, in the middle of the fourth quarter, and the game was close. The Knicks had turned over possession of the ball on the offensive end of the court, and Reggie Theus of the Kansas City Kings was on the fast break toward the basket— no defense, an open floor, an easy shot. Refusing to give up on the play, I hustled behind him to block the shot. As he went into the air for the layup, I planted my right foot hard and had started to elevate when I heard my right knee snap. Hurtling skyward in excruciating pain, I screamed, "Oh my God!"

I was at the pinnacle of my career and considered one of the two best forwards in the NBA. It had taken years of training and sacrifice to get me there, and I lived for the game.

As I came crashing to the floor, clutching my knee, writhing in pain, everything went hazy. The next thing I remember was a doctor confirming my worst fear: I had torn my anterior cruciate ligament; my career was over. In the history of the game, no player had ever successfully come back from this injury. I cried the rest of the night.

The next day, the Knicks went on to finish out the road trip, and I went home . . . alone. It had taken me twenty-one years to make it to the NBA. On the flight from Kansas City to New York, I vowed that I would be back, no matter what the doctors said.

I began by reading medical journals and interviewing five of the top orthopedic surgeons in the country. Three said I'd never play again. Two others believed I could. But only one of

Former NBA player Bernard King established a stellar basketball career in his fourteen seasons. The onetime New York Knick and New Jersey Net scored more than 19,000 career points and was a four-time NBA All-Star. Since his retirement, King and his wife have launched their own retail–wholesale business.

them, Dr. Norm Scott, believed his technique would allow me to return as an all-star.

My only moment of self-doubt came after the surgery. I had forty-one metal staples in my knee (which was bigger than my thigh), and my leg muscles had atrophied to nothing. It would take months just to learn to walk again. But the day I came home from the hospital I began working with a physical therapist, breaking down the scar tissue and rebuilding my strength. The pain was intense; even the neighbors could hear my screams. My doctor said that swimming would help. And so, facing my lifelong fear of water, I showed up my first day at the pool ready with my life jacket to practice in water three feet deep!

I was on a mission. For two years I worked out with my physical therapist five hours a day, six days a week. I gave her the seventh day off and worked out alone, driven by a sign on my wall that declared: I SHALL NOT BE DENIED.

The pain I endured was the breaking of a shell that led to a deeper understanding of myself and the world. I believe that success comes to those who work hard, are well prepared, and believe they can overcome any obstacle in life.

Against all odds, I returned to the NBA, and in 1991, with a rebuilt knee, I was the oldest player in the starting lineup of the All-Star Game. I shall not be denied. ■

"I vowed that I would be back, no matter what the doctors said."
—Bernard King

Johnnie Cochran

SUCCESS IS NOT just about making lots of money. For me as a lawyer, success is about changing things. I became a lawyer largely because of one of my heroes, the late Supreme Court Justice Thurgood Marshall, who made major inroads as a civil rights attorney prior to his high-court appointment. He used the law to change society for the better. In my own way, I want to achieve a similar goal.

Throughout my career I have been involved in civil rights cases against the Los Angeles Police Department—my nemesis, because we have always been on opposing sides of various lawsuits having to do with racial justice. During a two-year period, seventeen young men were killed because officers were misapplying or mis-

using a restraining practice known as the choke hold. Because the police were using it only on Blacks and other people of color, my legal team filed a lawsuit. In the 1982 case of *James Thomas Mincey III* v. *The City of Los Angeles,* we won, and the choke hold was banned. James Mincey died as a result of the choke hold. We proved that although officers were supposedly trained, many of them still didn't know what they were doing —and had been misusing the choke hold, which renders the body involuntarily sluggish, for far too long. Now the police can't just stop someone for a traffic offense and use the choke hold. They can use it only in life-threatening situations. Since the moratorium on the choke hold in Los Angeles, no person of any color has died as a

Johnnie L. Cochran, Jr., has earned a reputation as an outstanding trial lawyer, often combating police brutality and many other equal rights cases. Long before his success and national recognition during the O. J. Simpson trial, he challenged injustices and negotiated record settlements for clients. He serves on a host of legal and community organizations and has received notable awards. His autobiography, *Journey to Justice,* became a best-seller.

result of its use. Even though Mr. Mincey lost his life, he saved the lives of many others.

The police also used a hog-tying procedure whereby they would handcuff a suspect's arms behind his back, tie his legs together, hook the legs up to the handcuffs, and lay him down. A large person hog-tied can suffocate from lying on his stomach. Since this vile procedure was often used on people of color, we were ultimately successful in having it banned as well.

I've spent all my adult life preparing so that when the opportunity to foster change came along, I'd be able to step up to the plate. Many people work very hard throughout their lives to prepare themselves and then lose the courage to move forward simply because

they're afraid to fail. But in order to achieve success, you have to discard fear. I've had to conquer my fears to bring attention to what I perceive as injustices toward our people, people who helped to build this nation and deserve the best that it has to offer.

My dream has always been to affect and transform my community. It's powerful to bring about change, but we have to be mindful of what the great Frederick Douglass said: "The one thing about power is that you have to be willing to speak truth to power." I believe we always have to speak truth to power and never be afraid to fail. Only then will we be free and forceful enough to effect change—and that is how I define success. ∎

Hezekiah Walker

IN ACHIEVING FAME and success, loneliness has often been my companion. But on my journey, it has been faith that has sustained me. It has kept me going during times when there weren't any answers to my questions. As a child, I always wondered why my family had to be living in the projects with no father in my home, no money, none of the up-to-date clothes all the other kids had. I didn't look at the bigger picture. I was looking only at my immediate predicament, but somehow my dreams and hopes for success never died. I believed that one day I would be bigger than my problems if I held on to my faith and set myself apart from the crowd.

I paid the price of being different. You might say that my faith didn't cost me anything. After all, the things I missed were mostly negative. But when I was a child, I didn't see those activities as negative, I saw them as *the* things to do. Hanging out was the thing to do. Back then robbing and stealing were the things to do. If you didn't smoke weed, you weren't down with the crowd. So I went through a period of loneliness, feeling as if no one my age understood me. I felt like an outcast. But deep down I knew that if I wanted success and fame, it was going to cost me some-

thing. Instead of doing what my peers considered cool, I did the opposite. I didn't turn to drugs; I didn't rob and steal; I didn't become another statistic. I held on to the truth of my faith.

Daring to be different got me cast out of gatherings, friendships, groups, and parties. I was never invited to the places that most young men went. Other kids probably said my being different was being weird, but I looked at it as being unique. All I wanted to do was sing gospel music and go to church. In those days, no one thought that gospel music was for young people. Church was not seen as the place for a young, cool brother. But I kept telling myself that there has to be something special about you if you want to succeed.

Now after a few years of success in gospel music and doing what I love most—pastoring and preaching—I've realized that the more rewarding things in life don't come easily. That's the most important lesson we Black men have to understand: If we are going to have anything, we have to work for it. And if that means paying the price of loneliness, pay it, but never lose faith. Today I take care of what I have. When you pay that special price for success, you're going to protect it, cherish it, love it, and appreciate it. ■

Pastor of the Love Fellowship Tabernacle Church in Brooklyn, New York, Pastor Hezekiah Walker, founder and leader of his Grammy Award–winning choir, is credited as one of the leaders of the contemporary urban gospel genre that blends modern R & B with traditional gospel. Using music as part of his ministry and outreach, Pastor Walker has become a teacher and mentor to today's younger generation.

CHOICES

First, feel, then feel, then
read, or read, then feel, then
fall, or stand, where you
already are. Think
of your self, and the other
selves . . . think
of your parents, your mothers
and sisters, your bentslick
father, then feel, or
fall, on your knees
if nothing else will move you,
 then read

and look deeply
into all matters
come close to you
city boys—
country men
Make some muscle
in your head, but
use the muscle
in your heart

—Amiri Baraka

Damon Wayans

Comedian, producer, and writer Damon Wayans began his television career as a featured performer on *Saturday Night Live* and went on to achieve success with the Emmy Award–winning 1990s series *In Living Color*. He stars in television's *Wife and Kids*. His film successes include *Bulletproof* and *Mo Money*, which he also wrote and executive-produced. Wayans is the author of the best-selling book *Bootleg*.

WHAT STANDS OUT about *In Living Color* is that it was truly my family's television show, based on the sense of humor that we developed during our childhood. My brother Keenen, as executive producer, was the filter and sounding board for our comedic ideas. Even Jim Carrey's comedy mirrored our sensibility of what was funny. Keenen didn't dictate what Jim did, since we were like one big family, and we all saw things the same way. It was hard work, but it was a great experience to spend the night in the office and know in the morning that we had created something really funny. I was on the show for two years, and it was fantastic just coming to work and seeing my family.

When we left *In Living Color,* I saw how strong a family we were. While doing the show, we made a huge amount of money—more money than we had ever made in our lives. But Keenen was unhappy with some of the politics behind the show and he said, "I'm out of here," which basically meant, "*We're* out of here."

Leaving really challenged our love for one another. We had to ask ourselves, "Is it *we?* Or is it *you?*" I didn't have to leave, because Fox offered me the executive producer spot, which showed the company's lack of respect for us as brothers and for our family's devotion and loyalty to one another. I would have had Keenen's blessing to go ahead and take advantage of the opportunity presented to me, but in order for us to make a serious impact and statement, I knew we all had to leave.

I didn't have to think about the decision long, because I didn't care how much money they offered to pay me. I knew that if I couldn't look into my brother's eyes and share the love that we had developed over the past thirty-something years, it wasn't worth that opportunity. No amount of money was worth it. I am proud of that decision. It was a statement to our family, and to those who were watching, that we Wayanses move as a team. ■

Ben Carson

Benjamin S. Carson, Sr., M.D., earned a reputation as a surgeon of extraordinary talents in 1987 after he led a seventy-member surgical team that separated twins joined at the head at the Johns Hopkins Children's Center. As director of pediatric neurosurgery since 1984, he also holds appointments in the departments of neurosurgery, oncology, plastic surgery, and pediatrics at the Johns Hopkins School of Medicine. He has received many honors, including more than twenty honorary doctorates, and is sought after as an inspirational speaker. Dr. Carson's autobiography is titled *Gifted Hands*.

AS A YOUNGSTER, I was a very poor student until my mother made us start reading books. Initially I started reading about people, animals, plants, and rocks. I gravitated toward the scientific realm and began reading about physicians and surgeons, and that changed my image of who I could be. Most of the adults around me worked in the factories in Detroit. If they managed to get themselves a nice car and a reasonably nice house, they were very happy. As my image of myself expanded, I began to understand that the person who controls who you become is you, and that it's based on a series of choices you make and how hard you're willing to work on yourself and toward your goals.

My life reached a major turning point when I was fourteen. I had become enraged with another teenager and I tried to stab him with a large camping knife. The boy happened to be wearing a large metal belt buckle under his clothing, so fortunately, the knife hit the belt and broke. Had he died or been seriously injured, I would have gone to jail or reform school instead of college and medical school. I locked myself in the bathroom, and I prayed. I asked God to do something about that temper of mine. I realized that people who are angry all the time are people who put themselves at the center of the equation, which means everything is always aimed at them. There are people who never look at things from other people's points of view. I began to see that this is a sign not of strength, but of weakness and machismo. Also, it's saying that circumstances and other people control your emotions, and I refused to allow people and situations to have that kind of power over me.

I decided to take myself out of the center and began to look at things through others' eyes. That outlook had a profound effect on the rest of my life. Now it's very easy for me to understand a different point of view and to see where others are coming from. This has made a tremendous difference in my life and my relationships.

I've been inspired by Jesus Christ, and I try to remember his humble greatness and strength. Everyone is a valuable individual. That conviction has basically controlled my life. It also helps me realize that there is a power greater than we ourselves. ■

Malik Yoba

MY DAUGHTER WAS born when I was thirty. I consciously chose to have a child out of wedlock, because my daughter first appeared to me in a dream. In the dream I was pregnant and gave birth. But the love and adoration I felt through those visions of my child couldn't prepare me for the reality of fatherhood. Since her birth, I've been exposed to the many joys and challenges of raising a child. There's so much to the experience, yet there's no awareness of the multitude of issues men go through as parents.

During my first two years as a father I was operating on two levels: On the public level, I saw the potential for me to use my celebrity to communicate through various media outlets the many issues facing fathers. On a personal level, I was fighting for custody of my daughter in family court, in an environment where there are so many men without a voice. It was a crazy juxtaposition.

Family court is almost surreal. People were making all kinds of assumptions about why I was in court: Some thought I was making a film, while others thought I was there because I wasn't paying child support. People were constantly asking for autographs. Meanwhile, I was there trying to establish my right as a parent, trying to withstand numerous false allegations—from being accused of physical and sexual abuse to being called incompetent and a drug addict. I had to sit in court and listen to people say slanderous things about me.

That court case felt like my own personal civil rights battle because I had to maintain my composure while I was under verbal attack. In the courtroom, I couldn't express my outrage or protest. I had to speak through my lawyer. I spent thousands of dollars on legal fees for something that was fundamentally my God-given right—the right to father—when that money should have been going directly to my daughter. Rightfully, the court awarded her mother and me joint custody.

Although I've faced many challenges in my life, the struggle for custody of my daughter was my toughest obstacle. It inspired me to work to change the discriminatory conditions men face as fathers. That struggle has helped define me as a man. ■

Actor and activist Malik Yoba has received national recognition for his work and advocacy for youth causes. He uses the same energy and creativity in his television and film career, which earned him three NAACP Image Awards for his work in *New York Undercover.* Yoba's film credits include *Cool Runnings,* in which he made his film debut.

Robert Townsend

I FELL IN love with movies when I was a kid. I watched everything on television—all the movies starring Humphrey Bogart and James Cagney—but I never really noticed any Black people. My love of show business and desire to act inspired me to join the Experimental Black Actors' Guild in Chicago at fourteen or fifteen as the youngest member. Once I got into the theater, I looked at television and movies differently. I started to watch with a more critical eye and thought, *Why are Stepin Fetchit and Mantan Moreland talking this way?* At that time there was only one Black actor I saw who was dignified, powerful, and defiant: Sidney Poitier.

By the 1990s, I'd finally made my mark in Hollywood, making movies and doing television projects. One night I was at an awards dinner, and I ran into Sidney Poitier. At first I felt starstruck, but then I collected myself and told him that I enjoyed his work and how he had inspired me. He asked, "Why don't we get together and have lunch?" Without hesitation I said, "I would love to."

That was one offer I followed through on. I called him, and he invited me to his house in Beverly Hills. It was a regally beautiful house with wrought-iron gates with little spirals on

them. After he greeted me, we went into the dining room for lunch. We had salmon; I can still remember the plates and everything. It was an incredible moment.

After lunch we sat down and began to talk. I was so excited, I felt the adrenaline rushing through me; I was sitting with true royalty, a legend of legends. I told him how much I had idolized him as a kid—and still do to this day—because of his dignity. Finally I asked him: "Man, how did you accomplish dignity in the movies back then?" He looked at me as I continued, "With everybody else having to shuffle and buck, how did you escape it?" He simply said, "It's the power of saying no. They offered me a lot of different roles, but I haven't done that many movies, because I always exercise my option to say no."

That one afternoon reinvigorated and recharged me for a long time. In show business, we need to have a higher tier of professionals—the elders who pass on the wisdom and knowledge. Because show business is such a cutthroat industry, it's rare that our elders are able to survive in style and able to create a substantial body of work. Sidney Poitier has managed to do that. I hope I'll be able to do it, too. ■

Robert Townsend is one of today's most multifaceted and innovative talents. Wearing one or more of his various hats, the actor, producer, writer, director, and comedian exercises his innate sense of comedy and storytelling to create bold, entertaining works. His groundbreaking film effort was the 1987 satire *Hollywood Shuffle*, which he cowrote, directed, performed in, and financed (primarily with credit cards). His other feature film work includes *The Five Heartbeats* and *The Meteor Man*. Spurred by the success of his HBO specials and Fox's *Townsend Television* variety series, Townsend created the long-running WB series *The Parent 'Hood*. He was also a force behind MTV's *Carmen: A Hip Hopera*.

Forest Whitaker

Forest Whitaker, one of Hollywood's most accomplished actors and directors, has showcased his talents in a multitude of demanding and diverse roles. He has appeared in such successful films as *Platoon* and the Academy Award–winning *The Crying Game*. He received the Best Actor award at the 1988 Cannes Film Festival for his role as jazz legend Charlie "Bird" Parker in *Bird*. His 1993 directorial debut with the HBO movie *Strapped* earned him Best New Director honors at the Toronto Film Festival. He went on to make his feature film directing debut with the box-office hit *Waiting to Exhale,* following it up with *Hope Floats.*

I GREW UP in a very religious home. My grandfather was a southern Baptist preacher, so every Sunday my parents made me get up and attend church. When I was about eleven years old, I started to question the whole notion of religion. I even started reading books about different religions. Whenever the Jehovah's Witnesses or people from the Nation of Islam came to our door, I always had little debates and discussions with them. Occasionally I asked my grandmother Estella Strange some philosophical questions about religion, but she was firmly entrenched in her beliefs and didn't like my raising issues that contradicted her teachings. At her church, before the preacher delivered his sermon, he would reference my discussions with my grandmother and scream, "Sister Strange's grandson, could you please stand up?" Because my parents were there, I had to get up.

After I started reading more and asking questions, I used to argue with my mother and father about going to church. I would say: "Why is it that I have to believe what you believe? Why are you forcing me to get up?" Finally my mother said something that I've always respected and used in my life. She said, "You don't have to go to church with us, you don't have to go to our church at all. You don't have to believe in what we believe—but you have to believe in something. So you can decide if you want to go down to the Nation of Islam, or if you want to go to a Jehovah's Witness Hall, or to a Jewish Temple, but you're going to go somewhere."

That experience taught me that we should always be open to new ideas, but that ultimately there should be a philosophy that guides us. There should be core principles that you're passionate about and live by. And I've held on to that through the years.

To have purpose in our lives, we must believe in something. ■

Barry White

With his forty-year career going strong, Barry White has gone from singing bass for a 1960s doo-wop group to minting a catalog of gold and platinum singles and albums as an artist, writer, and producer. His soaringly orchestrated music and his instantly identifiable voice have made him known as the purveyor of musical romance and as the Icon of Love. White's autobiography is titled *Love Unlimited*.

IN 1960, I went to jail for six and a half months for stealing tires. I'd never been locked up before, and I couldn't stand it, but it was an enlightening experience. I had a brother who was constantly going to jail. He loved that kind of life, but I didn't. I vowed to change my existence—from trying to be a gangster, gang-banging, and all that silly shit. When I got out of jail on August 28, 1960, that's exactly what I started doing, turning my life around.

I'd been home for about two or three days when some friends said they needed a bass singer for their group and asked me to join. I told them yes and committed to rehearsals and learning the songs. I started really liking it.

When we finally went into the studio, I knew the recording business was where I would spend the rest of my life. I loved it that much.

We recorded a song called "Little Girl." It wasn't a hit, but it was a smash to me. Through our recording sessions, I saw a recording console and mixing board for the first time, and I learned what role everyone played—from engineer to producer to songwriter and singer. I met new people, learned new things, got involved.

I look at my early experiences—good and bad—as the impetus to get me on the right track. Since those days I've tried to stay positive and not let negative things rule my life. Time has been my greatest friend. It heals. It fulfills. ∎

John Lewis

THE TOUGHEST DECISION

At an early age, Congressman John Lewis from Georgia developed an unwavering commitment to the Civil Rights Movement. For more than four decades, he has been at the vanguard of U.S. human rights struggles. As a student, Lewis organized sit-ins at segregated lunch counters. In 1963, he became the chairman of the Student Nonviolent Coordinating Committee (SNCC), which he helped form. After serving on the Atlanta City Council at twenty-three, he helped plan, and was a speaker at, the 1963 March on Washington, and he led the 1964 March on Selma known as Bloody Sunday. In 1986, Lewis was elected to the U.S. Congress, where he has served seven terms.

THE TOUGHEST DECISION I ever had to make was whether to leave the Student Nonviolent Coordinating Committee (SNCC). I had been the chair of the organization for three years, and we had become a band of brothers, a circle of trust. It was a very dangerous period, and we depended on one another. Some of those young people, like Julian Bond, our communications secretary, and field secretary Don Harris became closer to me than my own blood family. They became two of my closest and dearest friends.

Leaving SNCC was like a separation or divorce. It was like cutting off a segment of my family— those brothers I had struggled and worked with. I had been involved in a movement with people I got arrested with, went to jail with, got beaten with, and almost died with. During our sit-ins at lunch counters, people would put lighted cigarettes out in our hair or down our backs, pull us off lunch stools, or beat us. We saw so many brothers attacked, shot, and killed, but we were like soldiers in an army, only with a dream that somehow and some way we could create the

beloved community. We made a conscious decision that we would not retaliate or engage in violence, that we would be orderly and peaceful.

The Student Nonviolent Coordinating Committee had been built on the philosophy of nonviolence and the idea of a truly interracial democracy, but the organization began shifting and laying aside some of the ideals that I held dear. There was a growing effort that was exclusionary toward Black Power, and I felt the organization was losing its soul and its mission. It was time for me to leave. I felt that if I had stayed, I would have been compromising my principles. Some members stayed while others left, but in spite of our ideological split, we've maintained our friendships even today.

We were true believers in the idea that somehow and some way we could change America. We believed we could make our country different and better for our people while creating a sense of community and family. So as I reflect on my lifetime of facing struggles and challenges, leaving SNCC remains as the most difficult decision I ever had to make in my life. ■

Nickolas Ashford

MY LIFE IS a rags-to-riches story. For me to be homeless in New York was God's way of putting me on the right track because that was when I learned to appreciate life and count my blessings. The experience taught me that freedom was my most valuable asset, and that success is doing the things that really make me happy. You can be happy in every aspect of your life. And that power comes from within.

When I came to New York from Willow Run, Michigan, my first idea was to be a dancer because I had studied dance at the University of Michigan. Of course, the sixty-four dollars I had in my pocket ran out very quickly. That's how I found myself homeless, sleeping in parks and on the subways for six or seven months until I eventually found my way.

I went to auditions and realized that I could dance, but I didn't know the dance language because I hadn't studied it. So I failed miserably at each audition. I realized this was going to be an uphill journey. I went on for months trying to find a job, and I discovered that I could live off twenty-five cents a day. In the 1960s, I would wash a window or do something that would earn me twenty-five cents. Then I could get two hot dogs and be satisfied.

When I was homeless, I learned how to be free and live off barely anything. So I decided not to give anyone eight hours of my time any longer and to work part-time instead. I realized that I couldn't possibly do the things in my life that I wanted to do by giving up that much time. I decided I'm happier when I'm working for myself or being creative. That's how I found my own happiness, because what I do now I would do for free. ■

Singer and songwriter extraordinaire Nick Ashford is half of the best-selling husband-and-wife music team Ashford and Simpson. As singers, Ashford and Simpon have produced fifteen of their own albums. As songwriters, the duo has produced twenty-two gold and platinum records, and earned more than fifty ASCAP awards for outstanding contributions to popular music. With a career spanning more than thirty years, Ashford and Simpson started as house writers for Motown and have expanded to owning their own production and music-publishing company. Nick Ashford is truly a musical legend in his own time.

Ed Bradley

MY FIRST TRIP to Europe, in 1969, changed the direction of my life because I saw something that I had only read about in history books and novels. In Paris, people were living together in a way that didn't seem to be race-dominated. It just didn't seem to be as segregated a society as the United States. I thought Paris was a much more civilized city than New York.

Europe opened my eyes to another way of life. I came back to New York to work for the next year and save enough money to live in Paris. That greatly influenced my future, because I ended up leaving Paris after two years of working as a stringer for CBS, then going to Vietnam as a reporter for the network. From Vietnam, I went to Washington.

Paris was a city not without its own prejudices. I found that opportunities there were restricted not so much by race as by class. But that was thirty years ago, and this country has changed a lot. There are doors open today that were closed thirty years ago.

In retrospect, I saw the rise of integration and participated in the integration of the media in this country. I covered Dr. Martin Luther King, Jr., on local radio in 1963 and 1964, and I went to the March on Washington. I lived through the sit-ins in the South and the Mississippi Freedom Ride. I'm very fortunate to have been born when I was, and to have seen the changes that took place.

When I was growing up in this country I saw no Black people on television. Today I travel this country for *60 Minutes,* and in virtually every local television market I see men and women of color. My first trip to Europe initiated global experiences that have opened opportunities for me to witness a changing world. It has been exciting to see and be part of history in the making. ■

After a lengthy career as a reporter, anchor, and White House correspondent for *CBS News,* Ed Bradley has been a principal correspondent and coeditor on television's top-rated *60 Minutes* for more than two decades. He has won the Robert F. Kennedy Journalism Award, the George Foster Peabody Award, and multiple Emmy Awards for his investigative reporting and prime-time specials.

Douglas Wilder

IF THERE WAS one moment that had a major impact on my life, it was when I heard the May 17, 1954, *Brown* v. *Board of Education* decision that banned race discrimination in schools. That Supreme Court decision was brought about by persons of color—men like Thurgood Marshall, the first Black Supreme Court Justice; Jim Nabrit, lawyer, educator, and civil rights advocate; and Spottswood W. Robinson III, who subsequently became the first Black federal judge appointed to the Washington, D.C., bench. They helped convince nine White justices to acknowledge that the Supreme Court had been wrong in the 1898 *Plessy* v. *Ferguson* separate-but-equal decision. That's when I realized there was a need for lawyers of color to be involved in our legal struggle for equality, and I decided to go to law school. I recognized that opportunities for Blacks could exist only if there were people fighting for them. Even though I was contributing to society, I was unhappy that I wasn't meaningfully involved in the fight for equality—and I knew I had to take action.

In 1990, Lawrence Douglas Wilder became governor of Virginia, the former capital of the Confederacy, becoming the first elected African-American governor in U.S. history. Wilder first made his mark on Virginia's political history in 1969, when he became the state's first African-American state senator since Reconstruction. He again made history in 1985 when he became Virginia's first African-American lieutenant governor. Wilder's accomplishments have been celebrated by several Virginia institutions that bear his name.

Despite my desire to go into law, there were certain variables I started to question: Did I have an adequate background to study law? As an undergraduate, I had majored in chemistry and later worked as a chemist in Virginia for a couple of years. There was also the race issue at work. At the time, I couldn't attend law school in Virginia because they didn't accept people of color, so I had to look at colleges out of state. Initially I was concerned about Howard University's accepting me because I hadn't majored in history, political science, or economics. Fortunately, Howard took a chance on me.

I'm indebted to those trailblazing lawyers who inspired me and whom I later came to work with and know personally. And I'm also indebted to Howard University for providing the forum that allowed that to take place. Because of Howard I was given a platform that has let me contribute in ways few before me could have dreamed of. I have seen and lived historic advances—and much still needs to be done. ∎

THE CIVIL RIGHTS MOVEMENT

You pay for it, for sure, don't let nobody tell you you don't. You pay. In all the ways possible, through the traps, moon light traps, collecting absences, and kisses, lovers trail through the imagination lighting fires throughout the civilized world, destroying primitive man's "progress" to the obeisances of spirit, the salary of the blind.

It is a path song. Mountains pass under and over, cold birds turn to blink. A rope hung from way up, tied to a leader, a spirit, a system, an old teacher himself, tied up higher movn just a lil higher.

Sometimes you want to know it is worth it. The deprivation, the trying narrow decisions, move on, move on. You want to know sometimes when the world beat down around you, the planet groans from so much pain, the pointless murders and idiot laughter from the merv griffin show. Then you know that what you do is what the ancestors prepared you for. The lighting of the flame.

The moving of the rock. The shouting out of the great names, the great national spirits. Then the feeling in tuned and turned slowly our turn itself hits a certain note, mighty pythagoras, the sound, the color.

—Amiri Baraka

Dennis Green

Dennis Green is consistently a winning football coach. He has had a distinguished career as head coach and vice president of football operations of the Minnesota Vikings, and has held coaching positions at Northwestern University, the University of Iowa, and Stanford University. With a mandate to give back to the community, he supports and donates his time to a host of community and charitable organizations and programs.

IN THE MIDST of the 1950s Civil Rights Era, I was born in the inner city of Harrisburg, Pennsylvania, the youngest of five boys. We lived through sad and harsh days, but I feel fortunate to have been around people who shared a passion for the cause of Blacks in America. My father died when I was eleven, and my mother died when I was thirteen, but they were great role models for my brothers and me. So much of my adoration of them came from the sacrifices they made trying to raise children while facing prejudice and discrimination. They made sure that we were aware of the foundation of the Civil Rights Movement and of what it meant to our future. They left a great blueprint for how to be a man and to live with a purpose.

I lived in an all-Black universe. As a ten-year-old, I had no understanding of what was going on outside of my world. I can remember my mother talking to me about the first march they held in Harrisburg, in 1959 or 1960, to support demonstrations taking place in Selma, Alabama. My mother explained to me why it was important for her to participate in the march and to support our fight for equality. It was important for her to fight the discrimination our people were suffering. When I entered high school in 1964, my credo was: Always do the very best you can, because brave men and women worked their tails off to move us forward. As an African-American, I felt I had a responsibility to get a good education and to go to college and give it 100 percent. If I played sports, I had to go all out.

That determination to succeed has been the driving force in my life. Now that I'm in my fifties, I pride myself on carrying on the fight for equal access, equal opportunity, and equal education. It's not a burden. I have the strength and the integrity to stand up to discrimination whenever and wherever I see it. I feel a responsibility to preserve the groundwork the trailblazers laid before us. I like exactly where I am right now. In this second half of my life, I've dedicated myself to carrying on the legacy of the civil rights pioneers—and my parents. ■

Tommie Smith

THE 1960s WERE a time of change, and I felt it was necessary for me to get involved, as a Black man and especially as a Black athlete. When I stepped off the playing field, my three-fifths-human status was completely reinforced. I was relegated to second-class citizenship and faced discrimination from White folks on the street and in the classroom. My fellow Olympic athletes and I decided that as world-class competitors we couldn't stay silent. We had to use athletics as an opportunity to let the media and the masses know that yes, we were there. Yes, we ran track. Yes, we ran fast. But our main goal was to win equality and social acceptance. The 1968 Olympic Games was the platform we chose to showcase our feelings.

It took two years to prepare for what we did in Mexico City. Our actions were highly organized. That's why we started the Olympic Project for Human Rights. One critical issue for the project was to exclude South Africa from the games because of apartheid. We were also fighting for the hiring of more Black coaches on the high-school and college levels, more women in sports, and more academic help for Black college students. And we put our lives on the line for those demands.

At the final Olympic Project meeting, we decided that the victory stand was the place for each Black athlete to do what he or she thought necessary to shed light on the unequal policies in

Olympic Gold medalist Tommie Smith is probably best known for his silent "Stand for Victory" during the 1968 Summer Olympics in Mexico City. Following his track-and-field career, Smith went on to play professional football with the Cincinnati Bengals. He was later appointed to the faculties of Oberlin and Santa Monica Colleges. He is a member of the National Track and Field Hall of Fame.

Opposite page: Tommie Smith (center) and John Carlos (right) make their silent protest during medal ceremonies for the 200-meter race at the 1968 Olympic Games in Mexico City. On left, Peter Norman of Australia.

our social system. We wanted to make sure that our actions showed that we were winners on the field, but social losers once we got back home.

By proudly holding up our clenched fists in the Black Power stance, we made the "silent gesture heard around the world." We said nothing, but our social and political agendas were put forward on the world stage. People had a chance to see and think for themselves because we said nothing. Other athletes staged their own idealistic protests: Some wore socks or tams that they removed during the national anthem. Five athletes, including Kareem Abdul-Jabbar, refused to compete in the Olympic Games. But people remember the two athletes with the raised fists because it was such a strong gesture. That act of defiance was my bold call for social

awareness and social change, and I couldn't imagine that the fallout from it would drastically affect my life.

For a time after the 1968 Olympics, I was fired from every job I held because of the stand I took in Mexico City. Even if I was washing cars, I'd get fired. I had to leave California to find a job. So I relocated to Ohio and continued my education and received my master's degree. I ended up as an instructor at Oberlin College. Nine years later I returned to California. I applied for many positions throughout the nation. Fortunately, I received a call from the Santa Monica College academic board and was hired as a faculty member and head track-and-field coach. Finally, I felt I had come full circle and that my actions in 1968 had not been in vain. ■

Conrad Muhammad

IN THE 1960s, the United States saw the emergence of the Nation of Islam and Malcolm X, the Black Power Movement, and the Black Panther Party for Self Defense. I'm fascinated and inspired by that period, because those young people no longer said, "Okay, we'll follow the elders." Instead they said, "Now we can formulate a new social and political philosophy and provide leadership for our own generation." It was a passing of the torch. That era also included the drama at the 1968 Olympics in Mexico City, with John Carlos and Tommie Smith making their silent Black Power protest. Black people were really connected with one another. We knew what we had to do to make progress.

Our brothers and sisters stopped being polite—we weren't asking White people to empower us or to love us. As a people, we were simply affirming that we're here, we're Black, we've been struggling for a long time, and we now intend to take full advantage of the Voting Rights Act, the public-accommodations bill, and all the other advances that the Civil Rights Movement has produced. During this era Blacks knocked down the doors to corporate America, to academia, and to the media. An unprecedented number of Black television shows proclaimed Black awareness and addressed Black issues. Unfortunately, once we got inside, by the mid-1970s, we got polite again, and the momentum dissipated. That's where we are right now.

I am disheartened to hear Black people say that nothing has changed in America. That's like saying W. E. B. Du Bois, Paul Robeson, Dr. King, Malcolm X, and Huey P. Newton all failed. The conditions today are different, so the

Minister Conrad Muhammad has been considered the political voice of the hip-hop generation. He became the Nation of Islam's spokesman to youths and students before being appointed leader of the historic Mosque #7 in Harlem. Seven years later Minister Muhammad left the Nation to found A Movement for CHANGE, focusing on bringing the voice of the hip-hop generation to the political arena.

challenge for my generation is not simply to duplicate what's been done, but to look at the problems in society today with the same commitment our forefathers had. Because we still have a long way to go, many Blacks are reluctant to acknowledge the progress that has been made, thereby robbing the Movement of its momentum.

In this political and social reality, one never reaches the mountaintop because there is no mountaintop. There is a continued fight and struggle among the various constituencies in this country for empowerment, and it's up to each of us to continue and to understand that the struggle for affirmation and empowerment in America is a never-ending one. As long as we remember the lessons of Elijah Muhammad and Malcolm X and the other great ones who offered us a vision, I think we're going to be all right. I'm very optimistic about the future. Blacks are going to become major players in this society— much more so than we are today. ■

"Now we can formulate a new social and political philosophy and provide leadership for our own generation."

—Conrad Muhammad

Kareem Abdul-Jabbar

After a twenty-season, record-breaking NBA career, Kareem Abdul-Jabbar is still considered one of history's greatest basketball players. Inducted in 1995 to the Basketball Hall of Fame, he was the first player to score 37,000 career points. He won the Most Valuable Player Award six times and was selected for the All-Star Game seventeen times. He has been the NBA's all-time leading scorer in regular season and playoff points. Since his retirement from basketball, Abdul-Jabbar has been involved in the entertainment industry, acting in feature films and television shows. He has written four books, including his autobiography, *Giant Steps*.

IN 1964, BETWEEN my junior and senior years in high school at Power Memorial Academy in Manhattan, I worked for the Harlem Youth Authority program, called the Har You Act. The program was the brainchild of Dr. Kenneth Clark, a renowned and beloved educator, who believed that education was the key to the future for Black youth. The program offered classes in dance, drama, photography, and music, and we had a band. I wrote for a newspaper we published in our basement offices at the YMCA.

That summer, Dr. Martin Luther King, Jr., came to speak to the program participants. As a member of the journalism workshop, I had the opportunity to interview Dr. King after he addressed us. There were reporters from the major media outlets who asked Dr. King all kinds of barbed questions, but the only thing we wanted to know was how the youths in Harlem could help to attain civil rights for *all*

Americans. This story was covered in *Jet* magazine; so I appeared in *Jet*—way back in the picture with my head peeking over Dr. King's shoulder.

I had been carrying the weight of bitter hostility inside me because of the previous year's church bombings in Birmingham, Alabama. That horrific event had left me feeling enraged and powerless. I'll always remember how Dr. King helped broaden my perspective to really understand what we were trying to accomplish in the Movement. He inspired me to use my voice, whether through journalism or my unique platform as a basketball player, to express nonviolent outrage in our civil rights struggles. Because of Dr. King, I was able to formulate ideas about how I could help our people move forward to a better position in society. I managed the anger that I felt in my youth by speaking out on civil rights issues and participating as a way to influence change. ■

Marion Barry

IN JANUARY 1965, I went to Washington, D.C., to run the office of the Student Nonviolent Coordinating Committee (SNCC) there, after running the New York office for about four months. The 1960s was a period similar to Reconstruction during the 1860s and 1870s, when there were efforts all over the country to scandalize and discredit Black leadership. One very dramatic event I witnessed during my early years in Washington was Adam Clayton Powell, Jr.'s, removal from Congress.

Adam was one of my heroes. Before him, I had known nothing about Black, big-city politicians or congresspeople because there weren't any in the South—not in my birthplace of Mississippi, or anyplace else. When I came to Washington, Charles Diggs organized the group of Black representatives that later became the Congressional Black Caucus. The earliest group included John Conyers, Louis Stokes, Bill Clay, and Shirley Chisholm—a handful of Black congresspeople. But none of them were from the South. Imagine our southern states, where all these Black folks lived, and not one representative came from South Carolina, North Carolina, Virginia, Mississippi, Florida, Alabama, or Georgia.

The House of Representatives had refused to seat Adam as a congressperson because of a host of allegations, but it doesn't really matter what the charges were, since when people want to discredit you, they say or do whatever it takes to vilify you. A man who came to work for Adam gave damaging information about him to the House Committee. Adam was upset and hurt to be betrayed, and he was deeply pained that despite all he had done in Congress, his colleagues would exclude him from his congressional seat. He sat in his office and cried. I didn't expect that, because we were taught that men shouldn't cry. Adam always gave the outward appearance of being so strong and courageous, but that day he cried and drank a couple of shots of liquor. Then he went out on the steps of the Capitol and made one of the most dynamic speeches I've ever heard. I was in Adam's office with several other people, and we discussed his riveting speech. He wasn't crying; he wasn't whining. He was articulate. He displayed a powerful sense of courage and determination.

Eventually, the allegations against Adam Clayton Powell, Jr., were overturned by the Supreme Court. But his very tough experience, which I was a witness to, helped and encouraged me when I was facing my own political adversities. I've had my share of challenges, and my faith and Adam's strength and determination have kept me grounded. ■

From president of his college NAACP chapter to SNCC's first national chairman to four-term mayor of Washington, D.C., Marion Barry has served his people for more than forty years. In 1971, he went from grassroots activist to elected official after winning a seat on the school board and the city council. In 1978, in a stunning victory, Barry became Washington's mayor. After serving three consecutive terms, Mayor Barry hit the lowest point in his political and personal life after being convicted for falling prey to illegal substances. But in 1994 he made a triumphant return to Washington by winning an unprecedented fourth term as mayor. He has in recent years taken a new career direction with a financial investment firm.

John Conyers

Serving more than thirty-five years in Congress, U.S. Representative John Conyers, Jr., from Detroit is the second-most-senior member of the House of Representatives and was the first African-American Democratic leader of the House Committee on the Judiciary. He was a founding member of the Congressional Black Caucus and the author of several bills signed into law, including the Martin Luther King Holiday bill, the Alcohol Warning Label Act, and the Victims of Crime Act. Congressman Conyers also introduced a bill that would require the study of racial profiling by the Justice Department and one that considers the feasibility of reparations for African-American descendants of slaves.

OVER THE YEARS, I have had the privilege of working with leading civil rights figures, men who faced incredible danger to help move America forward. Today I realize what an awesome experience that was. The people who came together in this struggle were heroes—they put their lives on the line—and they must not fade away into the shadows of history.

The Civil Rights Era was a defining moment in which America began to change. Segregation had to be officially declared illegal, and racism could no longer be sanctioned, overtly or covertly. The danger attached to these challenges made civil rights workers real revolutionaries, and there was nothing to protect them. In many instances, elements of law enforcement were actually working against them. Change was brought about by African-American leaders who persuaded their governments and other people of goodwill that they had to do something. Men like Dr. Martin Luther King, Jr., Andrew Young, and Ralph Abernathy were visionaries who faced some incredible obstacles in the effort to help Blacks achieve equality. I never knew just how brave and valiant they were until I came face-to-face with the evil they were trying to purge.

When Dr. King was jailed in Selma, Alabama, Mrs. King asked me to come down and bring a congressional delegation. We were able to get a government aircraft to transport members of Congress. Once we arrived in Selma, we held huge press conferences, meeting with the sheriff and other authorities, trying to get Dr. King and his people released. One night we were holding meetings in a church when cars started circling outside. We turned off all the lights and hid under the pews until the cars left, because this was a time when racist folks would not only shoot into a church, they would set it on fire. While we didn't encounter any actual violence, the threat of it was in the air, and it was seared into my consciousness that a church was no sanctuary from our opponents. I have a great respect for the African-American church because it produced so many leaders of the civil rights struggle. It fostered a connection between

having faith that we can make our situation better and getting actively involved in changing the system.

The more I reflect on that period in history, the more I see how brave Dr. King and others like him had to be to force America to change. They held on to their faith despite the daily battles they faced. I think the faith and hope of that movement has inspired much of the work I've done as a national legislator. It has shaped my outlook and formed the core of my philosophy.

As a member of Congress, today I face many of the same civil rights battles that Dr. King, myself, and others fought against more than thirty years ago. There are attacks on affirmative action, and the practice of racial profiling is tolerated throughout this country. Acts of hate are committed against our nation's citizens because of their race, religion, or sexual orientation; and particularly in the 2000 presidential election, many African-Americans, older Americans, and ex-offenders were disenfranchised in the voting process.

As a legislator, I have protested against these practices by introducing legislation to combat racial profiling and hate crimes as well as to restore voting rights to ex-offenders. I am actively working on electoral reform, so that all citizens can fully participate in the electoral process. Although these types of injustices still exist in America, the spirit of the Civil Rights Movement is alive and powerful. Many of our nation's citizens join me and other leaders in our fight against bigotry, and we will continue our work toward full inclusion in this society of all Americans, without condition. ∎

"I never knew just how brave and valiant they were..."
—John Conyers

Haki R. Madhubuti

I WAS BORN into apartheid America. The one advantage I had was a mother who read and encouraged me to read, and who did not allow me to acquire a victim's imagination, mentality, or personality. Victimhood as a hat was hanging heavy in the air as I entered adulthood in the 1960s, and a great many people were wearing it.

After I was released from the U.S. Army in 1963 and later heard of the murder of four little Black girls in Birmingham, Alabama, my life changed forever. I became absorbed in Chicago's Black Arts, Civil Rights, and Black Power Movements. As a young developing poet fresh out of the military, those movements saved my life. They gave my life greater meaning and a cultural purpose.

The struggle was about real democracy. The most pressing issues were to share governmental power at all levels, to open public facilities to all, to empower the disenfranchised with the vote, and to recapture and redefine Black images universally. We also were struggling for equal participation in the educational process, for larger living and working spaces for people of color, for redefinition of women's roles in a male-dominated society, and for the open and raw disclosure of the worldwide destructive powers of racism and White world supremacy.

These Black empowerment movements provided me and other young African-Americans of that period with a context for discovering identity and purpose. It also provided us with a posi-

An award-winning poet, publisher, and educator who was active in the 1960s Black Arts Movement, Haki R. Madhubuti (Don L. Lee) has published over twenty-two books, with more than 3 million copies of poetry and nonfiction in print. He is the founder of Third World Press. and his book *Black Men: Obsolete, Single, Dangerous?* has sold more than 1 million copies. Madhubuti is a professor of English and the founder and director emeritus of the Gwendolyn Brooks Center at Chicago State University.

tive vision for the future. The Movement prevented me from being swallowed by the lowest common denominator: street culture. Street culture is a culture of containment; it all too often leads to a dead end. It is a counterforce to Movement culture and, in today's urban reality, denotes survival at any cost.

In contrast, the Black Power Movement existed as an extended family, developing a culture that was productive and caring. Involvement in the Movement provided me with something to care about that was not insulting to my own personhood. It defined relationships and challenged me to rise above the limited expectations of others and myself. One of its major contributions was in the arena of ideas. We launched new magazines, publishing companies, independent schools, financial institutions, electronic media companies, and much more—all driven by a new emerging Black middle class with an entrepreneurial spirit.

The 1960s ushered in human rights for Black people, and we also took on a new attitude about ourselves. Many of us ceased being Negroes, became Black and African, and approached life as a series of possibilities. ∎

"Black empowerment movements provided...a context for discovering identity and purpose."

—Haki R. Madhubuti

LEGACIES

A closed window looks down
on a dirty courtyard, and black people
call across or scream across or walk across
defying physics in the stream of their will

Our world is full of sound
Our world is more lovely than anyone's
tho we suffer, and kill each other
and sometimes fail to walk the air

We are beautiful people
with african imaginations
full of masks and dances and swelling chants
with african eyes, and noses, and arms,

though we sprawl in gray chains in a place
full of winters, when what we want is sun.
We have been captured,
brothers. And we labor
to make our getaway, into
the ancient image, into a new

correspondence with ourselves
and our black family. We need magic
now we need the spells, to raise up
return, destroy, and create. What will be
the sacred words?

—Amiri Baraka

Tom Joyner

TWO PEOPLE, MUHAMMAD Ali and John H. Johnson, helped me define what would eventually become an ongoing theme, shaping the way I live and do business. When I was a DJ on a Dallas radio station, Ali was a frequent guest on my show. Eventually I even went to work for him. Sometimes we would drive down a busy street in a city, and Ali would stop his car, get out among the people, and sign autographs. He loved being around his people, loving them as much as they loved him. The Champ taught me that no matter how big or important some may think you are, you have to stay close to the people. He genuinely cared about the welfare of Black folks, and as much as Ali loved to brag about his boxing skills and how "pretty" he was, you've never heard him bragging about his generosity. Yet he has given millions of dollars to many charities and individuals over the years. He was a champion to thousands of people who would never have gotten a chance to actually see him box in the ring, simply because he had such a big, generous heart. He was and is The Greatest. Ali has been a constant reminder to me that my first responsibility is to make life better for others.

Later when I worked for my mentor, John H. Johnson, as the morning man on his Chicago radio station WJPC, I learned firsthand from the master the importance of advertising and marketing through Black media. When Mr. Johnson created *Jet* and *Ebony* magazines, he had to prove to the White media that Black people were consumers who should be valued. He included monthly surveys in his publications, asking people questions like: Do you own or rent your home? How much money do you make? What kind of car do you own? Before

Tom Joyner, the award-winning host of his own nationally syndicated program on ABC Radio, is known as the "Hardest-Working Man in Radio." His humor, intelligence, and hard-hitting social commentary have made him one of the most popular DJs in the country. He has received several professional awards, was inducted into the Radio Hall of Fame, and was named Man of the Year by 100 Black Men.

long, he had developed a database filled with valuable information about Black people. He took this information to the advertising agencies, proving that we do spend money on cars and homes and laundry detergent.

Next he told advertisers that if they wanted Black people to embrace their products, they needed to put Black people in their ads. If it had not been for Mr. Johnson, there would be no Pine-Sol lady. Thanks to him, Halle Berry is a spokesperson for Revlon, Grant Hill is a spokesperson for Sprite, and I'm a spokesperson for Southwest Airlines. I've even appeared in ads for Dark & Lovely although I'm light and bald! Mr. Johnson pioneered a battle that still hasn't been won. Black people spend billions of dollars annually, yet even now the Black media have to jump through hoops to get White advertisers to spend money on Black radio, television, newspapers, and magazines.

Recently, along with Tavis Smiley, our political commentator, I took many corporations to task for not spending money on Black media. I'm pleased to report that progress is being made. After a well-publicized standoff with CompUSA, the head of the company admitted that the firm needed to do a better job of reaching Black consumers and supporting Black media. He vowed to hire a Black advertising agency. This action means not just more revenue for Black radio, television, and print media, but more work for Black salespeople, copywriters, and actors who will appear, or be heard, in these ads. That's not just good news for Black media, it's good news for everyone. One week after CompUSA made its announcement, American Airlines announced that it, too, was hiring a Black advertising agency. Tavis and I have taken a lot of blows for bringing the advertising issue to the forefront. But back in the day, long before there was a *Tom Joyner Morning Show* or a BET, Mr. Johnson took on the advertising giants all by himself. They listened to him because he was right. And what was right then is right today.

The fight for parity on advertising spending for minorities is far from over. But I'm up for a good fight any day—The Champ and John H. Johnson trained me well. ■

Julian Bond

TWO OF MY most vivid childhood memories
are from photographs. The first picture hangs on
my office wall. In it, three men dressed in the
caps, gowns, and hoods of academia stand behind
two children, a boy and girl. I am the boy, standing in the middle. My right hand is held by my
father, Dr. Horace Mann Bond, the left hand by
Dr. W. E. B. Du Bois; between Dr. Du Bois and
my father is renowned sociologist and activist

Dr. E. Franklin Frazier. Next to me is my sister, Jane Marguerite. I am two. She is three. It is March 1942.

The three men are engaged in a mock ceremony, confirmed by a document signed by all three and witnessed by my mother, Julia Washington Bond. In it the three men, having "broken bread" and "after drinking pure water," dedicate the children to a life of scholarship, to seeking the truth, and to communicating truth to our fellows.

The second picture is horrific—I do not have or want a copy. But I can remember it better than the framed photograph and certificate I can see on my wall not six feet from where I sit. It first appeared in the *Afro-American* or *Pittsburgh Courier*—two Black newspapers that were constants in many Black homes after World War II, before there was an *Essence* or a *Jet*. It was a picture of Sergeant Isaac Woodward—tall, every inch the standard picture of a military man. His uniform was starched. The creases on his pants were so sharp they would cut paper. He wasn't standing erect, at attention. Instead, he slouched—decidedly unmilitary, even to a small boy's eyes. Where Sergeant Woodward's eyes should have been there were two large white patches instead. Sergeant Woodward was blind. And had this brave military man lost his sight defending democracy overseas in some gallant charge into no-man's-land? No, he lost his eyes in a different kind of service to democracy—or at least, in trying to demonstrate he deserved democracy's rights and protections. He was blinded by a policeman's nightstick when he didn't move quickly enough from the front to the back of a South Carolina bus.

I have no memory of the dedication ceremony that was carried out when I was two. The photograph is a prize reminding us of what is now a magic moment. Surrounded by my family and these giants, history put her hands on me. Sergeant Woodward, whom I never met, put his hands on me, too.

Years later, in 1961, in Albany, Georgia, the Reverend Samuel Wells told a mass meeting, "I can hear the blood of Emmett Till crying out to me from the ground." I can hear Du Bois and Frazier and Till and my family; I can hear Sergeant Woodward. They don't just call me. They call us all to service. It is a call we all must answer—each in his or her own way. ∎

As a founder of the Student Nonviolent Coordinating Committee (SNCC) and one of the major figures of the Civil Rights Movement, Julian Bond burst upon the national scene during the bloody protests and registration campaigns of the sixties. As an activist who has faced jail for his convictions, a veteran of more than twenty years' service in the Georgia General Assembly, a university professor, and board chairman of the National Association for the Advancement of Colored People (NAACP), he has been on the cutting edge of social change since 1960.

Opposite page (top): Dr. Horace Mann Bond, Dr. E. Franklin Frazier, Dr. W. E. B. Du Bois; (bottom): Jane Marguerite Bond, Julian Bond

Calvin O. Butts

The Reverend Calvin O. Butts's commitment to the enhancement of God's kingdom on Earth has manifested itself in his loyal attention to his community and congregation as pastor of New York's Abyssinian Baptist Church. He is involved in community initiatives such as homelessness, senior and youth empowerment, and ecumenical outreach, and is one of the founders of the Abyssinian Development Corporation, a community-based organization responsible for housing and commercial development in Harlem. He has spearheaded boycotts against racist policies and employment discrimination. Dr. Butts has received numerous awards and was appointed president of the State University of New York College at Old Westbury.

WHEN I ATTENDED elementary school at P.S. 92 in Corona, a suburb of Queens, New York City, there was a teacher named Mrs. Jackson. She lived in the community and was active in civic and social affairs. As far as I can remember, Mrs. Jackson was the only Black teacher in the school at the time, and she took an interest in me. She would say, "You're a bright little boy, but you're aggressive. I really need to have you in my class so I can straighten you out." She never had that opportunity; through fourth, fifth, and sixth grades, I was always placed in one of the other classrooms. Still, I never forgot her.

Years later, as a young man entering my freshman year at Morehouse College in Atlanta, I was surrounded by Black professors and Black administrators with a deep sense of history and commitment to the students. My years as a student at Morehouse, an institution founded in 1867 and having a proud and brilliant legacy, were the most definitive years of my life. On a social level, Atlanta was "all the way live," so I had a ball. Atlanta was where I first got into singer Johnny Taylor, and it was where I first met composer and producer Bernice Reagan of Sweet Honey in the Rock. I put on plays with her at the Magnolia Ballroom in that fine city. Adding to my political education, I met Black Power activists H. Rap Brown and Stokely Carmichael, and I worked for Horace Tate, who ran for mayor of Atlanta. My Black college experience was a rich one.

One night, I was at a concert in Archer Hall, which was the Morehouse gymnasium at the time. The school's glee club was singing "Lift Ev'ry Voice and Sing." I had heard people sing that anthem at different luncheons and banquets, but I'd never really heard it sung the way the Morehouse Glee Club sang that night. I remember standing there, my eyes filling with tears, then literally crying like a baby and saying to myself, *Mrs. Jackson, I finally made it to your class. I finally understand what you wanted to teach me.* ■

Michael Eric Dyson

A Baptist minister, best-selling author, and dynamic lecturer, Michael Eric Dyson earned a Ph.D. in religion before becoming a professor at several top universities. His books, respected for their scholarship and lauded for their popularity, include *Race Rules: Navigating the Color Line, Between God and Gangsta Rap,* and *I May Not Get There with You: The True Martin Luther King, Jr.*

I WAS PART of the Stanford Street gangs in Detroit, which my older brother Anthony and I joined when we were very young, probably nine or ten years old. Most young people join gangs to derive a sense of camaraderie, companionship, and protection in the midst of tough terrain. It gave us a sense of protection and ownership of our community and a feeling that we weren't alone as we faced moment-to-moment challenges in the inner city. It gave us a sense that we could make it and we wouldn't have to be targets of other neighborhood gangs that were seeking to claim our turf.

We had to pledge our fidelity to the gang and show that we were willing to fight to defend its principles. That meant we were going to be involved in some of the gang bangs and fistfights that were the necessary signs of our commitment. Unfortunately, most of the gang members are now in prison or dead. But relatively speaking, we weren't nearly as violent as the gangs are now. I didn't remain in that gang very long because I was a church boy and quickly learned that we had better images and better resources to make a decent life.

A most profound experience for me happened in the halls of the church. That's where I met my pastor, Dr. Frederick Sampson, who became my mentor and a most extraordinary male in my life. I was fourteen years old when he came to my church, the Tabernacle Mission Baptist Church of Detroit. I had been giving speeches and preparing oratorical presentations since I was eleven years old. So by the time I had met my pastor, I was already seasoned. He gave me a powerful and vivid image of what a responsible Black leader and minister should be to his people that has stayed with me to this day. He published my first piece in the church bulletin, a small essay I had written on the Black family. I accompanied him to many of his speaking engagements. He mentored and tutored me in the fine art of Black masculinity and manhood, and was certainly the central influence on my style of Black leadership and of joining the life of the mind with the life of the spirit.

I am honored to extend the fierce and proud legacy of Black preachers—tending to spiritual matters, upbraiding social and political injustices, and outlining the moral dimensions of Black progress. As I mature, I emphasize the need for spirituality over religion. For me, spirituality is the fundamental recognition of our common humanity in the quest of ultimate meaning. At its root, spirituality makes religion behave right. As a Black minister, I have a special obligation to speak truth to the powerful—and to the powerless. The powers that be seduce Black ministers with the carrots of material success, political access, and social status. But I resist the gospel of prosperity, which is often ahistorical and deeply opposed to the great religious and spiritual traditions that gained us our freedom. Instead, I support the gospel of justice and equality.

My decision to enter the ministry was a direct result of struggling with the best way to render service in light of my commitment to faith. And my own ministry and my roles as a public intellectual, as an ordained minister, and as a cultural critic have been fundamentally shaped in the crucible of my experiences. ∎

Richard Wesley

AS THE TWENTY- first century begins, it would seem that the Black male has become known more for his pathology and failures than for his dynamism, creativity, warmth, and yes, love. It is a notion that chafes—primarily because so many, including young Black males themselves, accept the idea of the failed and raging Black man. That I refuse to accept this idea I owe to a generation of men, both inside and outside my family, on whose shoulders I stand today.

Both my grandfathers, Richard Wesley in Shreveport, Louisiana, and James Thomas, Sr., in what is now Centerville, North Carolina, died before I was born. Both were the sons of slaves, born in the mid-1870s. Both remained married to my grandmothers for well over forty years. Between them, they fathered—and helped raise—more than thirty children. They had only grade-school educations but went on to become respected pastors in the Baptist church and the owners of their own land, which they farmed from early adulthood until death closed their eyes. They saw their children through segregated grade schools and sent them to all-Black boarding high schools. They did this without benefit of government loans, scholarships, Pell Grants, or philanthropic gifts. They were not special. Many Black families of the time were doing the same things. What they were had to do with dedication, a sense of responsibility, pride in themselves and their families, a firm spiritual foundation, and a belief in the future for their children. They lived on in their surviving children—my parents, aunts, and uncles; and those values were passed down to my sister, my brother, my cousins, and me.

My father and his brother, Jesse, were the

Award-winning playwright and screenwriter Richard Wesley has written several feature films and teleplays. His early Hollywood successes include *Uptown Saturday Night* and *Let's Do It Again.* His television works, such as *The House of Dies Drear* and *Mandela and DeKlerk,* have been recognized for their fine analysis of the human experience. As assistant professor in dramatic writing at New York University, he has shared his knowledge with a new generation of writers.

only Wesley men who came North; thus I have never known the Wesley side of my lineage as well as I should have. They were laborers who valued education, despite limited opportunities in their own growing up. My earliest memory of my father is of his reading every night when he came home from the factory, no matter how tired he was. My love of reading and learning came directly from him. Above all, my father and my uncle were both gentlemen, with an easy sense of humor, a quiet air, and a sense of dress and style that often set them apart. They treated women with respect and kindness, valued friendships, and had a personal honor about them that was hard to ignore.

My mother's brothers and sisters left the South, one by one, during the Great Migration of the Depression years. They settled mostly in the mid-Atlantic states, and I saw them all nearly every month of every year I was growing up. My mother's five brothers were the same kind of men—quiet, confident, and easy to be around, focused and loving. All of them had their foibles and weaknesses, but their positive qualities far outweighed their negative ones. It was easy to want to be like them, to imitate their style, their manner of speaking, and the way they treated those around them. They were hardworking men who stood by their wives and children, worked in their churches, and stood tall in their communities—just like my dad.

Those special occasions when I could be around my father, his brother, and all the brothers-in-law at family functions were incredibly magical times. Those men were like giants, and even years later, when I had grown taller than all of them and they had grown older and slower with age, I still felt great awe, love, and admiration for them. I feel fortunate and blessed to have had them as role models. ∎

Charles Floyd Johnson

A former lawyer, Charles Floyd Johnson decided to pursue his lifelong love of communications and the arts and headed to Hollywood, where he has become a powerhouse as a producer in film and television. He has earned several Emmy Awards for his work with *The Rockford Files, Magnum P.I., Quantum Leap, B. L. Stryker,* and *JAG.* He is also a founding member of the Media Forum and has worked to combat negative media images of minorities.

WHEN I WAS a teenager, my father told me stories about his days in the cavalry in North Africa. He would also tell me about Black men who were pilots in World War II. At the time I didn't really understand, because these men weren't mentioned in the history books. But my father had been so inspired by them that he even tried to become a pilot. It wasn't until the 1970s that someone gave me a book about the Tuskegee Airmen. I read it voraciously, and I remember saying to myself, *These are the men my father told me about. These were the men who impressed him.*

Ironically, years later George Lucas asked me to develop a feature film project about the Tuskegee Airmen. I thought I had been given manna from heaven, because you always hope you're able to develop projects that have a connection to you in some way. This was such an important story—one that would have made my father proud. I started traveling around the country to meet and interview them. I went to their conventions, to a number of air shows, and I got to know them personally.

What I found most fascinating was that in 1940 and 1941 these men were college students or recent graduates who went into the Army Air Corps. They came together for common goals: an incredible desire to serve their country and to fly. Some of them had even taken flying courses, and they did exactly what they set out to do. The Tuskegee Airmen actually got to go overseas and escort bombers into combat in World War II. So in 1948, when President Truman integrated the armed services, the Airmen felt their important roles in World War II helped to advance the cause of civil rights.

I spent hours talking to, and getting to know, a number of them, including Percy Sutton and General Benjamin O. Davis, who were very kind to me. They became my mentors and spiritual and emotional advisors. When my father passed away, they helped guide me along. These were very special men—men of great spirit. They had a joie de vivre about them. And they were passionate about the film, because they wanted to show the country and the world what their experiences had been.

We didn't get to make a feature film on the Tuskegee Airmen, because around the time we were preparing a script, HBO did it. I was still ecstatic, though. I thought, *Finally, their important story will come to life, and it will be brought into millions of people's homes.* ■

Henry Louis Gates, Jr.

WILLIAM EDWARD Burghardt Du Bois, the great African-American scholar, was the most important person of the twentieth century for me. In the late 1800s, W. E. B. Du Bois became the first Black to receive a Ph.D. from Harvard; he was one of the founders of the field of American sociology. He was our first professionally trained historian of the African and African-American experiences. He was a founder of both the Niagara Movement and the NAACP and edited its journal, *The Crisis,* for twenty-four years. He was the éminence grise of the Harlem Renaissance and the Civil Rights Movement and throughout his life brilliantly fought against racial discrimination and for the full participation of all Black and poor people in American society.

In 1909, he conceived of the *Encyclopedia Africana,* a comprehensive history of the peoples and cultures of the African diaspora. He was a staunch opponent (with Bertrand Russell) of the use of nuclear weapons. He published sixteen books and thousands of pivotal essays. As the father of the Civil Rights Movement, he did more than anyone both to redefine American democracy over sixty years of the twentieth century and to vouchsafe the rights of our people.

Du Bois was "the man," we might say; and just as Phillis Wheatley was the person of the century for Black people in the 1700s, and Frederick Douglass in the 1800s, Du Bois was indisputably the person of the century in the 1900s. We, his collective heirs, at our best are mere shadows of his towering genius, his commitment, and his integrity. ■

Professor Henry Louis Gates, Jr., is a leading African-American scholar and a formidable intellectual force in the field of Black culture. At Harvard University, he was appointed the W. E. B. Du Bois Professor of Humanities, chair of Afro-American Studies, and director of the Du Bois Institute for Afro-American Research. Among his many literary works, he counts *Africana: The Encyclopedia of the African and African American Experience* (which he coedited) and *Wonders of the African World,* the book companion to the PBS/BBC television series he hosted. Before joining the faculty of Harvard in 1991, he taught at Yale, Cornell, and Duke Universities.

Wyatt Tee Walker

MY CLOSE ASSOCIATION with three preachers of the gospel—Samuel DeWitt Proctor, The Reverend Vernon N. Johns, and Martin Luther King, Jr.—principally shaped my life and ministry. All three are icons of the African-American religious experience. Their names are recognizable wherever there is sensitivity to the struggle for human rights and liberation for African-Americans.

Sam Proctor, whom I met during my senior year at Virginia Union University, was the first minister I had ever seen break the strict, conservative dress code among ministers—he wore a sports coat and pair of unmatching slacks. His persona was far removed from the black suit–white shirt stern countenance I had encountered in my early life as a preacher's kid. I enrolled in his ethics class as a challenge to the newfound agnosticism that had led me to abandon my childhood faith for a time. In a single semester, Dr. Proctor awakened in me the awareness that I was called to the ministry. As a chemistry–physics major, I found that my new consciousness turned my life and aspirations for a medical career completely around. After graduating magna cum laude with honors, I embarked upon

seminary training the next fall with Sam Proctor, who, having received his Ph.D., was named the new dean.

Three years at the feet of this modern Gamaliel—the first-century Jewish scholar and teacher—instilled in me a thirst for both knowledge and excellence, and I finished the School of Theology as his protégé, summa cum laude. Proctor literally placed me in my first church in Petersburg, Virginia, while instilling in me the penchant for serious scholarly pursuits.

During my Petersburg years at Gillfield Baptist Church, an intimate relationship was forged with that great spirit, Vernon N. Johns, Martin Luther King, Jr.'s, predecessor at Dexter Avenue Baptist Church in Montgomery, Alabama. Reverend Johns was forced out of the pulpit at Dexter because of his uncompromising and radical social theories on the emancipation of Black people. His wife, Altona Trent Johns, came to Virginia State University with her outstanding musical gifts, and Reverend Johns, without a pulpit, accompanied her. This is where our lives intersected. I was greatly enamored of Reverend Johns and his legendary preaching prowess. I was fascinated and beguiled by his elephantine mem-

Wyatt Tee Walker, appointed as senior pastor of Harlem's Canaan Baptist Church in 1967, enjoys a distinguished record as a theologian, human rights activist, and cultural historian. Reverend Walker's prominent career has included being a former chief of staff to the Reverend Dr. Martin Luther King, Jr., pulpit minister at the historic Abyssinian Baptist Church, and a special assistant to New York governor Nelson Rockefeller. He is also a composer of sacred music and an authority on the music of the African-American religious experience, with a doctorate in that area. He is the author of more than twenty books.

ory and broad scholarship in so many disciplines. I followed Reverend Johns around like a puppy chasing a red wagon. Reverend Johns's bombastic style and radical approach to social change and his economic theories of Negroes changing their parasitic existence in America to economic productivity and independence did not make many converts. More than once I heard Martin Luther King, Jr., say that Reverend Johns created the climate of discontent in Montgomery that enabled him to do what he did with the fabled Montgomery bus protest in 1955.

King and I met as seminarians. Our relationship was casual until the Montgomery bus protests, when civil rights became an international cause célèbre and Martin Luther King, Jr.'s, name became a household word in the United States. We started to develop a deeper relationship in 1956, when he founded the organization that was to become the Southern Christian Leadership Conference (SCLC). During a 1957 SCLC meeting at Clarksdale, Mississippi, America's full-blown nonviolent leader named me to his national board. The rest is history. Our close alliance grew, and in 1960 Dr. King named me as the first full-time executive director of the SCLC. In the four years that ensued, the SCLC became the pivotal civil rights force that prompted the Public Accommodations Act of 1964 and the Voting Rights Act of 1965, monumental achievements induced by the campaigns of Birmingham and Selma.

In King, with his nonviolent armies across the southland, I saw the birth of a new spirit in people of African ancestry. Under his leadership we learned to channel our energy and rage against racism into protest and resistance, girded by faith in the crucified carpenter from Galilee. We must take pause to understand that King was no reformer. He was a revolutionary under whose aegis the system of segregation, buttressed by law and custom for almost a century, was completely dismantled—in less than a decade and a half! The great lesson I learned from him is thoroughly biblical: "Greater love hath no man than this, that a man lay down his life for his brothers and sisters."

It was through close association with these three African-American giants that my ministry took shape and has flourished for five decades. With their guidance, I have been able use the gospel to create my own legacy of self-empowerment and productivity for future generations of African-Americans. ■

Robert Van Lierop

MORE THAN THIRTY years ago, in 1967, I arrived in Dar es Salaam, Tanzania. It was my first trip to Africa, and I was excited because I had met and become friends with Eduardo Mondlane, the first president of the Mozambique Liberation Front. Eduardo was an incredible person who had undertaken a lot to help free his country from Portugal. Even with all his responsibilities, he was willing to lend me a helping hand. When I got off the plane, I discovered that my suitcase was lost. Eduardo and his wife came and met me at the airport with extra clothes. I was wearing the typical flashy clothes of the day: blue bell-bottom pants with white stripes and a white shirt with a long pointed collar. Eduardo laughed and said, "These clothes may not be your style, but I hope they'll do." It was such a gesture of kindness on his part, and it meant a lot to me.

When Eduardo told me the story of the revolution in Mozambique, I knew it had to be documented so that the world would know the story. I returned four years later to go behind the front lines and film the Mozambique freedom fighters in action. My friend Bob Fletcher and I spent six weeks in the war zone filming and documenting the struggle. What resulted was a film called *A Luta Continua* (The Struggle Continues). Neither one of us had ever made a film before. We were fortunate that the Mozambique Liberation Front embraced the idea and took us into liberated areas and the war zone so that we could get footage.

We lived and marched with a column from the guerrilla army. Inside Mozambique, the guerrillas had no vehicles—no jeeps, no trucks, not even bicycles. They went up and down mountains, across rivers, and through the bush on foot, carrying their supplies, equipment, and

Attorney Robert F. Van Lierop began his career as an assistant counsel for the NAACP before briefly leaving the law field to produce independent films concentrating on conditions in southern Africa. Van Lierop served as the ambassador to the United Nations representing the South Pacific island nation of Vanuatu for twelve years. He now concentrates on his private law practice and is active in numerous professional and civic organizations.

weapons. At one point, the Portuguese colonial army launched an offensive, deploying helicopter gun ships and dropping troops into the bush around us. This was a full-scale attack to try to wipe out this column. Some of us got separated from the rest of the group, and we zigzagged around banana trees while helicopters chased us, firing machine guns. We would hit the ground every few feet, taking cover until we made it safely into the forest.

Eventually we headed toward southern Tanzania, where the base camps were maintained. Tanzania was itself a poor, developing country, yet the people there sacrificed so much for the liberation of Mozambique, and also for the liberation of Zimbabwe, Namibia, and South Africa. That experience always stayed with me and helped set the tone for my work with other people fighting for their political independence.

Almost three decades later, I was decorated by the president of Portugal with its highest civilian award. It was given in recognition of my anticolonial work in East Timor. What irony, to be decorated by the president of Portugal many years after living with the freedom fighters in Mozambique. ■

"We zigzagged around banana trees while helicopters chased us, firing machine guns."

—Robert Van Lierop

Bill Cosby

Bill Cosby has entertained generations with his comedic genius and acting. From his Emmy Award–winning and barrier-breaking role in the 1965 *I Spy* television series to 1984's *The Cosby Show* and later *Cosby* in the 1990s, to his certified gold and platinum comedy recordings, and his phenomenal book sales, he has conquered all fronts as an actor, a comedian, an author, and a heralded philanthropist.

GROWING UP, I lived in the Richard Allen Projects in North Philadelphia. Above us lived a large man named Oscar Glover. This gentleman was a role model for us, and we didn't even know it. This was a man who took it upon himself one day to say, "We ought to start a Boy Scout troop." In my family we didn't have money for a scouting uniform for me, but Mr. Glover got an okay—I guess from the Boy Scouts of America—that whatever part of a uniform a boy could purchase was good enough, as long as he had *something*. In meetings, some kids just had the neckerchief, some had the shirt, some wore the short pants, and some had bought the full outfit—though I don't know how their parents did it. Most of us boys just had pieces of the uniform. I remember all I could afford was that neckerchief and later a shirt.

For us kids coming from the Richard Allen Projects, not having complete uniforms could have challenged our spirit. It could have been embarrassing. But Oscar Glover didn't get embarrassed; he made it okay. His focus was trying to mold us by boosting our spirits and our lives.

One day Mr. Glover said, "We're going hiking." We got up at six o'clock in the morning and packed our bags. Those who couldn't afford the Scouts' hiking pack had to carry their food in a paper bag. We didn't have a hired bus to take us up into the hills, fields, and mountains of Pennsylvania. No sir! We got on the Number 23 trolley car at Tenth and Parrish and wound up in Fairmount Park, right in the heart of the city. We marched, following Mr. Glover, around the edge of the park, and then into the park, never losing sight of automobiles and people sitting around with their lunches. Then we stopped, put our flag down, and tried to make fires and do nature-type activities. Mr. Glover did not get embarrassed, so neither did we.

With many of us today it is the uniform and what the uniform means to us that's important. Do you have two diamond earrings? Do you have two tattoos? What is the correct brand name of sneaker? Today people think: *This is my uniform, and I am somebody because of this uniform*. We were lucky that Mr. Glover didn't think that way.

People like Oscar Glover step forward every day. They're all over our communities, in the lower and middle economic areas, molding young women and men. They are male and female. These people give of themselves and don't ask for anything in return. That's why we need to salute them. To this day I still feel Mr. Glover's influence in my life. ■

Percy Sutton

IT WAS THE 1960s, just before the death of Malcolm X, whom I called Minister Malcolm. He called me Counselor. He was on trial in a New York municipal court in Queens County. The issue was whether Minister Malcolm had the right to continue to occupy the house in Queens that he had purchased when he was minister to the Black Muslim congregation.

After leaving court one day, I was riding in the front seat between two men. Both the driver and the other gentleman had .45-caliber guns in their laps, and the one on the right also had a rifle and a shotgun between him and the door. In the backseat, Minister Malcolm rode between two people with shotguns on each side and pistols in their laps. I turned around and asked, "Minister Malcolm, doesn't having all these guns and weapons around upset you?" He said, "No. It doesn't upset me. My people think I need them for protection. They think someone may kill me." I asked, "Well, how do you feel about it? Do you think it's protection? Do you think someone may kill you?" He answered, "Yes, and I don't think anything I can do will prevent it. Let me tell you this story," he said and told me the story of Omar, a Syrian slave.

A slave said to his master, "Master, oh, Master. Have I been a good slave?" The master answered, "Yes. You have been an excellent slave. One day you will be liberated." He said, "Well, Master, may I gain liberation now? I have heard the face of Death is seeking me. May I take with me the fastest horse that we have to escape?" For if he rode that horse by day and could make it to sunset, the face of Death would not be able to overcome him, and he would remain alive. So the master gave him the horse, and Omar began his ride. From early morning on the first day to sunset on the second day, he rode. He escaped Death. On the second day, with the horse well fed and watered, he began the ride at breakneck speed, and he completed the second day. Then, on the third day, with the horse refreshed, he began yet another full day's ride to escape the face of Death. It was just before sunset when all would be free for yet another day. There were seven paths down which Omar could travel with his fast horse. He started down the center path. He pulled up and backed out. He then decided to go down the path to the right of that. It would be known, if you're counting it from right to left, as the second path—number two. Then something told him to pull out of that one. Instead he chose path number six. He'd gotten only a small distance, less than a hundred yards down, when in the

middle of the path stood the face of Death. Death said to him, "Omar? Omar, where have you been? For three days I've waited for you to come. Why did it take you so long?" So Omar met his end—the face of Death—on this third day down the path he had not intended to take.

Minister Malcolm said, "So, you see, Counselor, you can twist and turn, but there is a destiny for each of us. And it is down the path that we don't know. But death will come. So I can't be worried every day about death coming." Later that evening I asked, "You know that story you told me? What about the things you force upon yourself?" He responded, "Oh, I don't think you can jump out a window or walk in front of a speeding truck without thinking you're going to get killed. But even then, that is your destiny." Less than sixty days later Minister Malcolm was slaughtered at the Audubon Ballroom. It was God's will. All those guns couldn't protect him. ■

Ossie Davis

I GREW UP surrounded by love, bravery, and good examples of strong Black men. Among them was my own father, who was a leader, a protector of his family, and a defender of his people. The environment was potentially explosive since we were surrounded by Jim Crow segregation laws, and lynchings were not uncommon.

My father, who had taught himself the art and science of laying railroad tracks while doing time on a chain gang in Virginia, was holding down a job on a railroad in Cogdell, Georgia, where I was born. Laying tracks was a job the Ku Klux Klan thought should belong to White men, and my father and his coworkers heard that the Klan was going to confront them one evening. I was a boy just ten when I watched my father and the other Black men from the railway crew stand watch all night. Rather than disappear or sneak out of town because they knew the Klan had better weapons and resources, and none would spend a day in jail for killing them, my father and the other men decided to stay and fight. Those Klan members must have known what they'd be up against, because they never showed up. As I look back on those dangerous days, it's amazing that I never saw my father back down from anyone.

I later came to know as personal friends and role models men who embodied much of the qualities my father possessed—men like the great poet Sterling Brown; Alain LeRoy Locke, the first Black Rhodes scholar and one of the fathers of the Harlem Renaissance; actor and activist Dick Campbell; Langston Hughes, the poet laureate of the Harlem Renaissance; W. E. B. Du Bois, a father and grandfather of our struggle for freedom; Paul Robeson, athlete, scholar, lawyer, performer, and the voice and consciousness of the struggle; master strategist A. Philip Randolph, who taught us the value of labor organization; Adam Clayton Powell, Jr., our mighty prophet who taught us the importance of the Black vote and the Black dollar; Martin Luther King, Jr., who made spiritual the basis of our struggle; and the exemplar of manhood, Malcolm X. As a young man, I had my father and these shining examples to inspire me.

Black men—by the dint of hard labor, the sweat of their brows, and too often at the cost of their lives—have established a tradition of sacrifice, struggle, and overcoming what seemed like insurmountable odds. Thank you, Black men, who, as Sterling Brown says, "are strong men, who keep a comin' on, getting stronger." ∎

Ossie Davis has achieved stunning triumphs with numerous stage, film, and television credits. His rich body of work spans more than sixty years as an actor and writer. He wrote the critically acclaimed *Purlie Victorious* and is the author of three children's books and coauthor of a bestselling joint autobiography with his wife, Ruby Dee, titled *With Ossie and Ruby: In This Life Together.*

ABOUT THE POET

Amiri Baraka first gained notice as a poet and jazz critic in the late 1950s and has since explored a full range of literary genres—not only poetry and criticism, but also drama, fiction, and social essay. His artistic, social, and political evolution is reflected in his 1995 collection, *Transbluesency: The Selected Poems of Amiri Baraka/Leroi Jones (1961–1995)*. Born Everett Leroi Jones, Baraka established his reputation as a playwright with the 1964 off-Broadway production of *Dutchman*, which received an Obie Award. Baraka has received a number of other honors, including Guggenheim and Rockefeller Fellowships. In addition to being a professor in the African Studies Department at State University of New York at Stony Brook, he has taught at a number of institutions and has been arts director of the Newark Music Project.

PHOTOGRAPHY CREDITS

INDEX